Discerner

The End Of The Beginning

Brian Keith

Copyright © 2014 by Brian Keith

Discerner
The End Of The Beginning
by Brian Keith

Printed in the United States of America

ISBN 9781498419406

All rights reserved solely by the author. The author guarantees all contents are original and do not infringe upon the legal rights of any other person or work. No part of this book may be reproduced in any form without the permission of the author. The views expressed in this book are not necessarily those of the publisher.

Scripture quotations taken from the King James Version (KJV) – *public domain*

www.xulonpress.com

A Discerner

Collin Keith, 1971, Columbia SC, A discerner from birth, "Seeing the hearts of others, in all their glory and dismay"

Acknowledgments

I offer my thanks to my God, who has been the greatest Savior, Friend, and Father I could ever ask for. To my wonderful wife and five children whom I love so much, thank you for giving me the time to write this. I thank my friends, who love me for who I am. Also a special thanks to Caroline M, Karen H, Mike R, Brandon G, and Scooter. Last but never least my grandmother and mom.

Journal Entry: Salvation Day 31

What defiles a man comes from what's within his heart, not from what he consumes.

It is much easier to think that what we take in decides who we are. If we take in too much booze, we become drunks; if we use drugs, we become druggies; if we eat too much food, we are gluttons. But it's not merely what we do that defines us; it is who we are without those things that truly measure the person. These outward things are merely the support structure for the internal beast we try to hide from the world.

Only when we can see the heart of a man or woman can we realize the depth of lust, love, hatred, joy, or pain one can experience. These things come from within, and they are what defile a person, not the theatrical display of everyday nonsense he or she shows to the world.

The good wife dreaming of another lover is an adulteress, even without ever cheating. The man who abuses his children in secret but is a well-liked teacher at school is just a child abuser living an outwardly honorable life. The preacher who loves porn but speaks against it is a holy hypocrite.

We are not always who we portray ourselves to be. We are only what we are in our natures: detestable scavengers clawing our ways to the top for an imaginary victory, only to reach it and find we are lower than we were when we started. When we look behind, we see only the carnage of our travels, but the fight to reach the top is what we call life.

I am glad that fight for me is over, and I can finally live in the freedom of knowing who I was and who I am now.

Chapter 1
The End of the Beginning
Revelation 22:13

Oh, what sweet words to wake up to! Surely this was going to be the start to another extraordinary day. I heard the words coming from that soft, angelic voice that was so very familiar to my ears.

My eyes were still blinking from a deep and needed sleep, as I slowly tried to adjust to the light of this new day. Now, I not only heard her voice but I also felt her gentle touch on the side of my cheek, ever so slightly, as she continued to say those words over and over again right against my left ear; it was just in a whisper. "Wake up, sunshine; time to wakey, wakey. Wake up, my big strong man; it's a new day." That sweet sound energized me more than even that first cup of coffee.

Her touch was slight, almost a tickle. And then, with no warning, it happened, just as it had so many times before. I felt the fingers first and then the palm, as she smacked the right side of my cheek with enough force to turn it red.

What was at first from heaven now seemed to be from hell. Adrenaline rushed to my brain. My mind immediately reacted from the pain. I surged forward, up and out of the bed, to grasp her for some due payback. But she was off the bed and to the shower before I could get a hand on her. I fell back down with a pillow on my face, rubbing the side of it, not knowing whether to be mad at her or love her even more for just being herself.

I hear an immediate knock on the door, Sir are you okay? Do you need us? No I don't, thanks though I yell back, I can take care of this one myself?

Those security guys are relentless; I believe they can hear a mouse fart.

They are patrolling outside like Rottweiler's on steroids watching everything that moves. They are always looking out windows and chattering on radios every few minutes. I guess they have good reason to be cautious though; I have been shot once in my own home and I have received more death threats than anyone to date, including the president. That's at least what they say anyway.

I have finally just started to get numb to it and realize it is what it is. If you want to really know when you have a problem, it's when everybody does like you, not when many don't.

As far as that woman who just ran into the bathroom, her name is Ava and she is no doubt the love of my life. That uninhabited reckless

Porsche of women, so elegant, uniquely brilliant, wild stallion with a sense of purity about her I just can't put my finger on. All I truly know is I never want to be without her.

Where do they make women like this anyway—gentle and abrasive, loving and sinister all in one beautiful little vessel, just enough devil to be tough and rough so that in a weird way it all makes her charming? Well, regardless, they broke the proverbial mold with my wife; in fact, they smashed it.

As I lay in the oversized bed, recovering from the smack my face had just taken, my body seemed to become a part of it. It was almost as if I was being molded to it in some way. It was one of those thick, spongy mattresses, like those in the commercials on which they put the wine glass and then some woman jumps up and down on it without spilling the contents of the glass.

I realized now more than ever I was just like this bed—older and firm, especially in my beliefs, but way more receiving and accepting of others, flaws and all.

Isn't it curiously strange, I thought, how life gets you to where you're at presently? There are so many turns, angles, and stops you never saw coming, but yet you're there regardless. For me, I enjoy the curves and the different directions. I get bored easily with the straightness of the road. I guess it's because I was born as an unsettled soul, never satisfied and always looking for more. Maybe we are all like that in one way or another. I'm not completely sure, but I think we are uniquely created to long for something greater than where we are or what we have. Everything else does what it is born to do; it performs its role and then dies.

Well anyway it's way too early to be thinking about this stuff. I need to get up and get going.

We were staying at the Royal Suites in downtown New York City, and the amenities were plush to say the least. I had come to realize something, however. As nice as this room was—like all the rooms I had been in lately—was just not home.

Hotel life is absolutely not what it presumes to be; at least it's not for a family guy like me. At first it seems great: your beds are being made and the room cleaned every day. There is great food, and the locations are always central to everything. At first glance, it seems like a dream life, but there is nothing further from the truth. It is a life of emptiness and solitude much of the time. It's a life with beautiful scenery but no one to appreciate it with.

I soon realized this, for I found myself missing the dirty life of a family. I preferred the dirty family to the pretty scenery. Compared to this place, my home hardly seemed attractive, but I had come to appreciate the stained carpet and little flaws of my own house much more than that of the whitewashed walls of the well-furnished suites.

Don't get me wrong. The living conditions were superb, but it was the ambiance of my family I missed—the sound of little kids screaming and laughing, spilling crumbs all over as they run when they shouldn't. I longed for the smell of dinner, even if it was Hamburger Helper. I even missed rubbing my little boy's feet as he

The End of the Beginning Revelation 22:13

watched cartoons—cartoons I didn't even understand and couldn't imagine him getting anything out of. Where had Underdog and Mighty Mouse gone, or the Little Rascals and Three Stooges? I was so out of date. I guess these new cartoons just seemed stupid to me, because he sure stayed interested enough. Maybe they have some weird hypnotic code that draws in young minds, I thought, but it's probably more likely I am just out of touch with the kids.

As I lay there, I couldn't help but gaze out the overly large window of what seemed to be the penthouse suite at this place. I could see the sun slowly creeping up behind the first skyscraper in my view. Everything was turning different shades of red and orange as the light slowly dawned on this side of the world. What seemed strange to me was that the beginning of my day was the end of the day for other people; my beginning was their end, and if I didn't know what time it was and was looking out the same window, it could be either the beginning or the end.

Lately life had been at high speed, and I was just trying to remember how I got to this place. So much had happened. I knew I came to the hotel in a limousine from the airport, but it was the events that led to the limousine and this moment in time that I was struggling with.

I was five hours from giving a message to the largest crowd recorded ever to hear a sermon—or anything else for that matter. The security people outside were like Rottweiler's on steroids, watching everything that moved. They were always looking out windows an' chattering on radios every few minutes. I guess they had good reason to be cautious, though; I had been shot once in my own home, and I had received more death threats than anyone to date, including the president. At least that's what I was told. I had finally just started to get numb to it and realize it was what it was. If you want to know if you really have a problem, it's when everybody likes you, not when many don't.

I could hear the water from the bathroom as my wife was showering. I almost wanted to go in and get even with her. I would have liked to turn the cold water on her while she was washing her hair, but most of the times I had tried that before she had caught me before I could do it. I remembered the last time I had tried it she had caught me and sprayed me with the showerhead before I could get the deed done. I needed to think of something much cleverer to get a little payback this time.

Still lying in bed recovering from the trip, I moved my eyes from the window and began to stare at the picture sitting on the nightstand. I always carried a few pictures when I traveled, as they kept me grounded and reminded me of who I am. I really think they just made me feel a little closer to home. The picture was of my brother, two of my cousins, and me all sitting on a tree that had fallen out in the woods. It had fallen against another tree and made a log ramp that went from the ground up about ten feet. We all had these stupid, dorky, perfectly blissful grins on our faces. I was about seven at the time. One of the cousins and my brother were older, and the other cousin was a little younger.

I still wondered to this day where that time went. It passed so quickly, and I remembered only little pieces of it. Where was the line from innocence to worldliness? I couldn't remember passing over it, only that I did and I was the worse for it.

Looking back, it just seemed to have left so quickly—the purity of youth that is. I missed it, and even a glimpse of it made me smile. Now I was reminiscing of old days and my long-gone youth, but I could remember when all I ever thought of was the future. Now it seemed there was a balance between the past and what lay ahead. The older I got, the more unknown the future became, and it was not as exciting as it was when I was a child. The future then was something to anticipate, not something to worry about.

That innocence we once had was not that we didn't do anything wrong; it was that we didn't see anything wrong with what we were doing. Jumping off a bed and elbowing your brother was supposed to cause pain, but it was okay; that was the point. Scaring my eighty-year-old great-grandma by hiding behind the door when she came in after dark was not bad; it was hilarious. Those days were filled with running in the woods, sleepovers, Kool-Aid, and getting into everything that even resembled adventure. How I missed it! I quietly thanked the Lord for letting me have those few memories, memories that helped me see what I needed to get back to.

Okay, enough was enough; I had to get up for real now. Finally, I got up and knelt beside the bed and said a short prayer. I couldn't help but thank God for giving me time with my wife and kids. More than anything, I thanked Him for His willingness to spend time with me. I thanked Him for his Son's sacrifice and all the love and benefits I had received because of that sacrifice—His life for mine. Jumping back onto the bed, I opened the thick, tattered Bible and started reading my devotion. The Scripture said a man can show no greater love than to give his life for his brother, but I wasn't *His* brother. I was His enemy. Who loves an enemy but God Himself? He had given my family and me so much. I knew I had abused those gifts at times, but I cherished them as well. He sees my heart, the good and the bad, but that is what I found the most comforting: that there is no hiding with Him. He knows my all and still loves me in spite of it all. He still calls me His son, for Pete's sake.

After finishing the devotion, I looked at the next picture on the nightstand. It was of Ava and me and two of my four boys. We were at the beach at the end of a seven-day vacation. It was the best trip ever, at least up until then.

Those boys were all growing so fast; one of them was in high school now, and one was starting middle school. The other was still just a baby. In the picture he was still in Ava's belly. At the time the picture was taken, I had not even known it. The fourth son remains only in my mind, as he never made it from birth.

In case you are wondering, I am a follower of Christ. Thinking of my past when I was lost (spiritually speaking) is mostly regrettable, but since I started my relationship with Jesus, my past has become almost like a lighthouse, always on, showing me where not to go and where it is safe. It sounds corny maybe, but there are plenty of fuzzy days and memories, and those are the stepping-stones of my life.

These stepping-stones are all the events of my life, one after another, all leading up to where I am now. The farther I try to go back, the smaller the pieces always seem to get, but the stones always stay in view.

At that point in that New York hotel, I understood and remembered one thing above all others: even before my Christian walk began, my life seemed to get started only when I began making my own decisions.

I guess you can say that was when I came to an age of accountability. Before that age, my life was about everybody else around me. They were the ones making decisions for me; my life was theirs, not mine. I don't believe your stepping-stones begin in life until it becomes your life and no one else's.

Chapter 2

Jeremiah 1:5

The first stepping-stone for me was my dad's death. When that happened, my life seemed to take on its own meaning. It's strange how one life ends and another begins.

I had just turned fourteen, and my dad had picked up a car from the auction. He used to get cars cheap at the auction and then turn a quick buck. He was on his third wife by then, but I didn't remember caring at the time. What I do remember is him having a lot of cash on hand all the time, and I thought that was cool.

I was old enough to know better than to steal, but I didn't care about that either. In fact, it didn't bother me in the least. My dad would come home drunk and pass out. I would then sneak a twenty or so, as it was easy to do and he never remembered what he had anyway. At any rate, I thought it was fair pay for having a drunk as a dad. I remember him always wearing a suit and always making deals. He was a salesman (diamond carbide cutting tools, I believe).

You need to understand something about my dad. Being a salesman was in his blood. A true salesman is born and develops his art. It doesn't matter what he sells; he'll be successful. My dad's dad sold candy and cigars, and my dad sold tools, and this salesman's bloodline seemed to have been passed down to me.

A born salesman is a like a warrior. He is just made to make deals, just as the warrior is born to fight. It's in the DNA. As a warrior has an instinct to react or attack, so does a salesman. He knows when to listen or speak. He can read someone's moves and responses, and he knows how to lead someone up to the commitment to buy—the "kill," to use warrior terms.

My dad was one of the best at what he did, but being a drunk dulled his abilities. On this particular day, the car he got at the auction had bald tires. It was raining hard as he drove back, and he had just finished downing a pint of cheap vodka, which, by the way, does not go well with bald tires.

Don't get me wrong. My dad was a good man, very smart and ambitious, but he lacked planning and patience, and the fact that he was a functional alcoholic didn't help either. After three marriages, he was now forty years old and back in Columbia, South Carolina, starting over yet again. I was with my grandmother and aunt that day, coming back from the mall.

That day is still etched in my mind. As I said before, it was the end of the beginning for me. It was the end of his life and the beginning of mine.

As my dad was driving back to the house, his car hydroplaned into oncoming traffic, and an oversized truck plowed into it like it was a piece of plastic on the road. The car immediately exploded into pieces of debris that scattered across all four lanes of the highway. His car was hit with so much force it trapped him in the front seat with the dashboard pressing against his waist. The police showed up quickly, and as always every rubbernecker in the world was gawking and slowing down to get a peek at the carnage.

I wonder why is it as a society we pretend not to like bad things when our actions say the opposite. We watch cage fighting, as one guy pummels the face of another, and horror movies are as popular as ever and the bloodier the better. In NASCAR we love a wreck, and with football the harder the players hit the more we enjoy it. In regard to this particular wreck, it was more than just onlookers being nosy; they seemed to be drawn to the disaster.

As we finally passed by the scene, I could see his arm dangling out the side of the car, touching the pavement. The blood was slowly trickling down to the ground from his fingertips. Paramedics and firemen were working feverishly all around the car.

My grandmother "Memaw" and aunt didn't know it was him because we had never seen that particular car before. But I knew.

My grandmother said, "Poor person. I hope he or she is okay, poor family." But I knew who that poor person was, and that poor family was us. When I saw the arm, I knew it was him. It was not because I recognized his arm, but I sensed it from the inside.

Jeremiah 1:5

Some might think this was a gut feeling, but that is not what it was for me. What I mean is that I saw it from the inside, just as if I were there with a front-row seat. That was my curse, you see. At least that's what I called this ability of discernment.

Some people might call it a gift, but at that time in my life it was more like a nightmare then any gift. I realize now, though, it was actually a window to God Himself. I just didn't see it that way.

Let me give you the best description I can of this so-called gift of discernment. It is the ability to determine, not just the truth about a person, but also everything around that person and the situation. I am able to see the truth between the lines of pretense and lies. I am able to see the reality of a situation instead of the falseness. I can't see the future, but I can see the truth in a life and the past points of that truth in others' lives.

The truth in the car accident was not just about seeing his face. I knew it was him because I saw what led up to it, as well as how it happened. I can see the truth in people's eyes and through their lies and deception. Everybody is putting on a show, it seems. They try hard to hide it or distract from it with their actions and appearances, but I see the true person.

The reality of this is ability is it's not pleasant to realize that people are so depressed. People just seem to be devouring each other every minute, every second of every day. It's as if some vortex is sucking the life out of people, and the crazy thing is that it doesn't have to be that way. We can stop it; we just don't. In fact, we seem to thrive in it.

I see people with jobs, kids, and nice clothes all focusing on what they don't have or how they want to be, never realizing what they do have or who they are. The more they focus on what they lack, the worse the lies become. The bitterness and self-loathing makes me want to vomit.

Back then, more often than not, I just tried to avoid using this "gift" if at all possible. The problem was, and still is, I can't control when it happens or what I see. It just happens. It's as if I see everything, but I am only in a trance for a few seconds.

I hadn't told anyone about it at that time. They wouldn't have believed me anyway, and I really didn't want the attention.

Another issue was that I had been embarrassed many times when it happened. The TRUTH is raw and unsheltered; nakedness of the soul is the best description for it.

Growing up with this ability was difficult, but it made me grow up quickly. As a ten-year-old, it's pretty awkward to sit in church beside a deacon's wife and see her in my mind sleeping with a man who is not her husband. When she caught me staring in my trance, she just smiled and kept on praising the Lord with her hands held high. What a joke I thought religion was back then. I guess I still think the same now, depending on what you mean by religion.

It was even more awkward to be sitting in a restaurant and see my waiter shooting up heroin and passing out. I had grown used to these visions, but I didn't talk about them at all, as I didn't really know what to say or who to tell. In my mind that kind of truth was not to be talked about but to be put away under the mirage of the played-out, invisible life a person seemed to have. It was as if I were accidentally given something no one but God should ever have.

On that day of the accident, when we got home, it wasn't long before we got the call that it was my dad who had been involved and that he had died. The news hurt but not that bad. He really had not been around much of my life, so it was more like a distant uncle dying than a father. To be honest, I didn't know what it was like to have a father; he was more like a fill-in father from time to time. I really was not fazed too much by his death, but I do remember from that day forward I had my own life to live. It was my life, and I was going to live it for me. That day I decided I didn't need a father anyway.

A week after the funeral, I went to the house of my friend Chris. We had a normal friend relationship. We fought some, but we had a strong bond, a bond of knowing we were in the same boat. He was the first friend I ever told that I loved as a brother, and he felt the same for me. The other thing we had in common was we loved to party — drugs, alcohol, pills, girls, fighting. We were up for anything that helped us forget our lives and make us laugh. When I got to Chris's house, the two of us took off into the woods. There he gave me the first joint I ever smoked. I smoked half of it, and I realize now it was some junk ragweed, to put it in common terms (not very good pot). I remember the feeling of freedom, though, the freedom of making my own decision. After that day I made it a point to drain every bit of life out of every moment I could, one party at a time.

The problem I ran into, as we all do, is that what I thought was making me free was really sucking my real freedom away, a breath at a time. Every smoke, drink, and pill I took told me I was free from this life. That was the biggest lie of all. They were only trying to steal me away for themselves, devouring me in the process. We all die as martyrs, you know: some for a religion but most just for their favorite sins.

Chapter 3

Psalm 14:1

It seems comical to me that they call it high school. That fit me just perfectly, as that's exactly what I was most of my time there. I was high as a kite and loving every minute of it—well, maybe not every minute but most of it anyway. Let's just say I loved most of what I can remember of it and leave it at that.

By "loving" it I mean the social aspect, the drugs, girls, friends, and those kinds of things. Certainly I did not love my classes or what school is supposed to accomplish.

Fortunately, for me and many others, Airport High School in 1985 had a smoking area where all the undesirables hung out. I am sure the preps talked about us being there and how trashy we were, but we didn't care; in many ways we knew we were trashy.

Being trashy, whether you were a boy or a girl, wasn't so bad; it just meant we lacked morals when it came to depriving ourselves of things we wanted. If we wanted to cuss, we cussed; if we wanted to get high, we did; and if we wanted to have sex, we did that to.

Most of us didn't have much money, so we shared more than other cliques did, I think. We had to work together more to get things done because of our lack of funds, but that never stopped us. We were nice for the most part, and there is always a code you follow regardless of the group you're a part of. Our code was to have fun at any cost and never do it by ourselves unless we had to.

As a freshman everything seemed to jump right out at me, I guess because of the newness of it all. The jocks were the bullies as usual, but they didn't own those halls as you might expect.

The first day of school, two of the bigger guys went at it in the hall, slamming each other against the lockers and slugging it out with serious blows to the face and plenty of blood to be seen. It ended when one knocked the other out completely, and we all just split up when the teachers came running. The freshmen kept their heads down and eyes up. More than anything we were just trying to find our place in this cement jungle.

The druggies all knew who we were, and we bought and sold most of our products before the first period bell ever rang. It was like a flea market for anything you wanted. Acid, cocaine, speed, valium, pot—whatever you wanted, it was handy. This was also where you found out where the parties were, who went to jail, who was pregnant, and who was hooking up and cheating on whom.

One particular morning I had about fifty valium my uncle gave me to sell. I had broken them up into five per pack and sold all but one before the first bell rang. I had one left, and I was going to keep it because that night was the fair. I had a smoking hot date, and valium always helped when trying to get lucky.

As I was walking to class, Stewart ran up to me and yelled, "Collin, I know you got one left, so please hook me up man." I tried to say no, but he persisted and I finally gave in. There was just something about me that loved the sale more than keeping the product. I loved the sale even more than getting high; in fact, it was a high all on its own. I think it was because it made me feel needed; I had a purpose, even if it was providing drugs.

When I got to my first-period auto mechanics class, I no more than sat down when the VP came into the room and directly announced that he wanted Collin Keith to come with him. I stood up and grabbed my jacket and began the walk with him to his office.

As we walked, he watched me the entire time. I knew I was in trouble, but I was not sure for what. I knew I had sold everything, but this was still nerve-racking. Instead of getting scared, though, I decided to have a little fun with him. As I walked I put my hands into my pockets, and he immediately said, "What are you doing?" I answered, "Nothing. What are you talking about? And by the way, where are we going? What's this all about?" He did not respond, maybe because he thought I might run.

When we got to his boring office, he sat me down in a tight leather chair.

"Collin," he said in a lower-than-normal voice, "I know you have been selling drugs this morning, so I want you to just turn them over and make this easy."

In my mind I was thinking, you're a stupid man if you think I am admitting anything and going down this easily. This guy had no idea whom he was dealing with. Instead, I just blurted out, "You're crazy!" My denial was so good I believed it myself for a second.

"Empty your pockets, son."

"No," I barked back, "and I ain't your son."

"If you don't empty your pockets right now, I'm calling the cops, and they'll make you empty them with your parents here. Does that work better?"

Seconds seemed like hours, but I finally gave in. I realized that scenario was not going to go down well for anyone, so I said, "Okay but with one condition. If I do this and you don't find anything on me, I don't ever want you to do this again."

"Okay, you got it," he retorted.

As agreed, I emptied my pockets completely and laid a hundred dollars, mostly in ones, down on his desk. "See. Nothing!" I said.

"Where did you get the money?" he asked.

"My grandmother, is that okay with you?" I was going to the fair that night and closed my defense with that.

He immediately let me go, and two things happened after that incident. First, I never sold drugs at school again, and, second, he never called me out again.

I went to second-period class after all this had happened, and I was admittedly a little shaken up, knowing I had almost been expelled. How glad I was that Stewart had bought that last pack. I guess the sun does shine on all of us sometimes, regardless of our actions.

I arrived in class as if I had just escaped death. The full brunt of what had just happened was swirling in my head, almost to the point that I felt dizzy. I sat down in my seat, and for the first time in my life I was actually happy to be in school.

Robin, the hottest teacher in our school, was writing something at her desk and told us to be quiet until she finished. She was one of those people you could stare at forever. She was like a fine painting that intrigues to the point that you wonder how something could be so beautiful.

As I stared, waiting for her to begin, it started to happen. I could feel my mind pulling me toward another vision. I had been through enough today, and as the images came rushing in, I gripped the sides of my chair. Having these visions out of nowhere was sometimes like getting on a roller coaster and not knowing when the drop was coming.

As the images came clear, I saw Robin when she looked to be about eleven. She was at her home, it seemed, and playing normally as any child would. She was in the middle of a green, shag-carpeted hallway. I saw a man coming up the stairs and stopping as he got to her. The man grabbed her by the arm and pulled her into a room, as if she had done something wrong.

I saw the fear come over her face as he grabbed her, but she never spoke a word, almost as if she were in shock. I felt myself growing angry, as she was just a little girl and this man seemed like a bully.

When he got her into the room and closed the door with a click to lock it, he picked her up and sat her on the edge of her bed. With his dark eyes piercing right through hers, he said, "You know what to do."

She tried to turn away, but he wouldn't let her. She began to cry, but he didn't care. He just casually held his hand over her mouth and whispered in her ear, "Don't start that or else. You know what to do, or I will hurt you, your mom, and your brother; so don't push me, Robin."

I tried to pull away from the thoughts. It was too much; I couldn't take it. Luckily, I came back to reality as quickly as I had gone out.

I was seething with anger when I came back, not because of what I had seen as much as because I didn't understand why I could see this in a person's life. This freaked me out because it was always so very personal and tragic. Some times were worse than others, but always it was something the person did not share with anyone else, a secret that only that person and I were privy to.

The other thing I always wondered was why it was these particular people. Why did I not see into everyone's life? It's not like I ever did anything with what I saw anyway. I just felt bad for them most of the time. I almost always had a sense of empathy for the person, but to be honest I had seen so much that I had grown numb to it. What happened to Robin I had seen happen to at least a dozen others in my past visions.

These visions never seemed to have a rhyme or reason, and they always happened at the most inconvenient times. I would ask God all the time why I was seeing this and whether there was something I was supposed to do with it. I finally stopped asking and just dealt with it, as I never seemed to get an answer from the great OZ anyway.

Did I mention that Robin was very pretty? Yes, I am sure I did, but she was also very patient. She reminded me of pure beauty, like a one-of-a-kind work of art that was made to be admired. She wasn't flirty but had a humble and polished look all in one. This was not a common trait in my world, especially in this school. Some of the guys would make jokes about her and what they wanted to do to her. They would say it just loud enough to get a laugh but not so loud that she could hear it. The girls in the class didn't like her because of this and were more often than not disrespectful. Even with this treatment, she was ever so patient and always more concerned with the education than the satire of the class.

I didn't make fun of her. I thought she was great, and I learned more in her class than in any other. However, I could see past her crooked smile. I could see she was sad and searching for something she had not found yet. At first, I really just thought she was looking for a husband, but I found out later it wasn't a man she was desperately seeking but something much greater: peace.

When the last period of the day came, I was ready to go home, I sat down in class, and Mr. Lunker, who taught math, began. I am sure he must have won some award for being the most boring math teacher ever. He had hair coming out of his nose and ears but none on his head. I just wanted to leave, as my brain was all used up for the day. As he rambled on, I left mentally and was not listening to him at all.

I looked to my left, and Mici was hitting on Wendy as usual. Wendy was the best-looking girl in our grade. She was an all-American perfect student. She didn't do anything wrong. She was stuck up and the prissiest girl in the school, I thought.

Mici was the testosterone-infused bully. He had the Tom Cruise hair and perfect teeth. He was the sneaky football player who laughed when he cut you down, as if he were just kidding.

These two being together was something you could imagine at every school; they were the poster children for these stereotypes. His hitting on her was way too clichéd for me, and I saw it every day anyway. It was even more boring than the teacher, so I tried to ignore all of it.

As soon as I tried to pull away from their sexual antics, I felt it again—my mind pulling me off. Images were flashing through my brain of a family and a little girl in one beauty pageant after another. The mom was pointing her finger at her, saying, "Don't mess up."

The dad was bored and uninterested in anything but other women. I was then pulled to a scene years later in what seemed to be a large house. I realized this was Wendy the cheerleader's home. She was just finishing eating what looked like a large plate of food with her family, who were all at the same table. They didn't look very happy, and no one was talking much. They were just shoveling food into their mouths, looking at one another as if to see who would crack first.

Wendy finally rose from the table and went upstairs to her room without saying a word. As soon as she got to her room, she went into the bathroom and locked the door behind her. She stared into the mirror for several seconds as if something were dreadfully wrong. Then she leaned over the toilet and began to stick her finger down her throat until she vomited up everything she had just eaten. It was horrible to watch, as she seemed to be in agony doing this.

As she finished she looked into the mirror again. She showed off her stomach and brushed her teeth. The look of despair was all I could see as she gazed with sadness into the mirror, a mirror that I knew would never give her what she was wanting. This was one the saddest moments I had ever seen, and it was a side of her I never knew existed. To tell the truth, I didn't want to know it existed.

I was coming to realize something through all these visions; namely, that nothing is the way it seems with people. Everybody is hiding their darkness and acting as if they are doing great. What a joke.

Suddenly as I was pulled back from the vision into reality, I heard the teacher asking me a question, for the second time apparently and much louder. I had no idea where he was or what I should say.

Mr. Lunker finally yelled out again, "Collin, do you know the answer or not?"

Thankfully, I heard that beautiful, saving voice of my friend Ava from behind. Without looking up, she told me in a whisper, "Two to the eighth power." I blurted out the answer just as Mr. Lunker was about to scold me again. He looked shocked that I had given the right answer, but he quickly settled down and went on with the lesson.

"Thanks, girl," I whispered. Ava just smiled as always and gave me a little smack on the back of the head and quietly said, "I am tired of saving your butt all the time."

I had known Ava since I was five, when she had moved in next door. She was pretty bossy at first, but we became friends quickly. She was cute but in a tomboyish way—like a sister, if you know what I mean. She always seemed to stay away from the bad stuff that was going on and always loved going to church, which she did all the time. Ava often invited me to go to church with her, but she never preached to me about it much. I knew she really liked it, and it wasn't something she had to do but was something she wanted to do.

The bell rang. The day was over, but it had taken its toll, and I hoped the visions would hold off for a while. It seemed they were becoming more frequent the older I got, and I still found no rational reason for any of it; it was just depressing.

Thank goodness the weekend had arrived. When I got home that day, I started getting ready for a night at the fair with a fine little hoochie who was known to not be very good at saying no, if you know what I mean.

As I was finishing up and getting ready to leave, I looked out my window. It was right across from Ava's window. We used to talk to each other from our windows at night when we were younger but not so much now. As I looked I saw she was reading something. It was probably her Bible, but I couldn't tell.

I spoke out the window to her and said, "Whatcha doing tonight, Princess?"

She looked back and said, "Not much. What about you, Dark Knight?"

It sounds corny, but those were the nicknames we had for one another because that was what we played growing up. I was always the dark night, and she was the princess in the castle. My job was to protect her from all the enemies of the kingdom. I liked it when she called me DK, as it made me feel powerful; I think she knew it too.

I didn't want to tell her everything about the night ahead because I was a little ashamed about who I was going out with. I just said, "Going to the fair." Then I said, "What are you reading?"

She held the book up and said, "A romance and adventure based on a true story."

"What's the title?" I asked.

She turned the book around, and as I expected, it was the Bible.

"Romance and adventure huh?"

"Yeah," she proclaimed, "more than you would ever think."

"Well, you have fun with that. I am going to the fair. Are you going?"

"I am tomorrow," she said.

"Who are you going with?" I asked, though I wasn't really sure why I cared.

"Mici is taking me."

As soon as she said his name, I almost lost my breath for a second. "What?" I nearly shouted.

"I am just kidding, stupid. I am going with my friends, Kelly and Tonya."

I quickly started trying to be cool again, but it was too late. I had blown my cover a little. "Well, you have fun. See ya." I closed the window and was on my way.

Our state fair was always particularly thick with drunks and vagrants, but what I found most amusing was this was one place you could see a guy puking on one side of you and someone on the other side getting robbed, and in the middle of it all was a mom and dad with their five kids, trying to have a good time and knowing this was what they were coming to. The only other place I could compare the state fair to is the Waffle House on a Saturday night, which lacks only the rides.

That night my date was even more rebellious than usual. She had on a miniskirt and a tight top, and just to make sure I knew there would be no resistance later, she laid a monster kiss on me as soon as she got into the car. I saw her look back at her house as we drove off. I didn't realize until later that later things weren't quite as they seemed—as usual.

We got to the fair, and just as I expected the drunks and partiers were all mixed in with the perfect little family pictures. We laughed and wondered why anyone would bring their kids to this place, especially at night.

As we waited in line for the first ride, my date grabbed my hand and gave me a soft kiss on my neck. I knew for sure, then, this night was going to go as planned.

As soon as she stopped kissing me, she turned to look at something, and my mind started to pull in images. I had started to have a vision. Suddenly it pulled me back to her house before we left. Her father was somewhat drunk, it seemed, and was telling her how worthless she was. He said she was just like her mom, a slut. He tried to grab her arm as she ran out the door, but she slipped away. The screen door slammed behind her as she rushed down the stairs of her porch.

As I came back to the present reality, I couldn't help but think about what I had seen. To say the least, my desire to continue hitting on her was not the priority it was before.

These stupid visions always came at the worst time. The night was still young, and I was a scholar when it came to rationalizing ways to get what I wanted and convincing myself not to feel bad about it. However, I did feel the urge to tell her I thought she was a really nice person and not just because she was beautiful. I think she appreciated the comment. She laid another long kiss on me right in the line and said, "I can't wait to get you alone later."

What happened next was a blur. Suddenly, I felt a thud come across my side. I fell to the ground and then quickly sprang up, realizing what had just happened. There was a fight going on between two guys, and it had quickly made its way over to us.

These guys were going at it, and my date had barely gotten out of the way. The crowd moved away, and just as the two separated, one pulled out a gun and aimed it at the other. The crowd went crazy then, and everybody took off hysterically in different directions. I was frozen, and then, as quick as a breath, the unthinkable happened: he pulled the trigger.

The bullet pierced the chest of the other guy, and he dropped instantly as the force knocked him onto his back. The shooter, surprised at what had just happened, dropped the gun and took off into the chaotic crowd and was gone. The wounded man was lying near my feet. I could see the blood, and I could see the life slipping away from him as his face turned pale. In a matter of seconds, he went from having color to a pasty grey, and he was turning greyer every second.

I leaned down, not really knowing what to do but trying to help. I told him help was coming, but I wasn't sure it really was. He stared at me as if in that moment I was the most important person in the world to him, and then he asked me a ridiculous question. I thought it was at the time anyway, but now I realize it was probably the most important question he could have asked.

"Is it real? Is it all real?" He slowly breathed the words out.

I said, "Is what real?"

I wondered if he was just out of his mind at the time. Then in that split second my mind pulled into this man's past. The vision was rapid-fire, but it was mind-numbingly clear. I saw him as a child and then as a teenager—snapshots of events in his life is what it seemed like. I saw him get married with his closest friend as his best man. Then I saw him in the hospital with a baby, and finally I saw him finding a note in his wife's purse from that same close, lifelong friend. The note revealed an affair and asked her to meet him at the fair that night.

The man jerked me back to reality. With his face already turning to death, he grabbed my collar. "Is it real?" he said again.

"Is what real?" I gasped back.

Then with a peace he seemed to long for more than he had, he said, "Is heaven real?"

I didn't know what to say, so I just said the only thing I could: "I hope so!"

He closed his eyes at the end of my reply and slipped away as medical help arrived and pushed me away.

That night haunted me for many years to come. It was the first time death really confronted me as an inevitable event in my life. Why did I say, "I hope so"? I wasn't sure I believed in a place like heaven. I had always thought it was all silly and childish wishes. But that was before I had seen death so close. Before, I never thought about dying, only about living and living the best I could to the fullest. After that night, death continued to creep into my mind, and I wondered many times what it would bring when it happened.

After a lot of thought, I think I realized heaven is a place for good people, and I knew I wasn't good. I never had a problem realizing I liked bad things. The problem came when I started thinking those bad things might have a consequence.

CHAPTER 4

John 7:17

It was April, and there was only one month of school left. I couldn't wait to leave that place. It was fun while it lasted, but I was ready to graduate to something way better than this run-down school, town, and people. My dreams were much bigger than this rat hole.

By some miracle I passed English in the fourth quarter, coming up with a 70 to end the year. I think Miss Turner ended up giving me the few points I needed at the end just out of love, or more likely because she felt sorry for me.

Robin Turner and I had grown closer over the years, and knowing the things that happened to her as a child made me want to be nice to her, more so than to most others anyway. I think she knew I needed someone to be nice to me as well. It was almost as if she knew me in the same way I knew her.

School was finishing up now, and none of the teachers were really asking anything of us. I think they needed the break more than we did.

As a student, it was not until later in high school that I thought about the teachers having lives too, that their lives were not just comprised of being in class for me and the rest of the students every day—you know, taking care of all of us unappreciated adolescents.

I was relieved when I walked into Miss Turner's class that last day. She smiled at me and said, "You know you just did make it, Collin."

I could only smile, feeling proud even of my 70 grade. You see, for me it was never about being the best; it was just about making it.

"By the way," she spoke up, "I need to meet with you after class for a minute."

Great, I thought, more stuff to deal with. Still, I didn't think too much about it. It was the last day, and what was the worst that could happen since she already said I had passed?

After class everyone left, and I stayed back. Robin sat me down, and we had the strangest conversation. Even before the conversation, though, before class had ended, I had been reflecting on the year that had just passed. I started to realize the last couple of years Robin had seemed more at peace, and I didn't seem to be pulled away to her traumatic past as much.

Right before class ended that day, as she was speaking, I felt it happening again. My mind was pulled away to what seemed to be her current house. This was different from the other visions because she was grown up. All the others were of her childhood abuse.

There was a man there and a woman who apparently was his wife. They were all crying, and Robin had her hands over her face. I could see her saying yes to the man, screaming it as if her words were uncontrollable. I heard him ask again with a calm but loud voice, "Will you forgive him as you were forgiven?" She again said yes, again sobbing uncontrollably, and they all embraced. It was as if Robin had released something from her inner core, something that had been eating away at her for a long time.

When the bell rang and everyone got up to leave, I almost forgot to stay until Robin asked me to hold on. That was when this strange conversation began. She looked at me with the softest eyes; I have to admit I was infatuated with her to some extent.

She said, "Collin, I know you have struggled over the last few years, and I am not just talking about school. I want you to know, even after graduation, I am here for you, and remember there is hope for a better tomorrow."

This was getting really weird. I think she realized I was uncomfortable, so she said one last thing before she hugged me and I left.

"Collin, no matter what you have ever done or ever will do, no matter what anyone has ever done to you or you have done to them, there is a place to get a clean slate. There is a place for starting over."

I didn't ask her what that place was, even though I wanted to. I wanted to leave even more, and she knew it, so she just hugged me and said good-bye.

That voice, that peace, and the solitude she had bewildered me. As I walked down the hall, I was mesmerized thinking about it. I wanted to scream out, "Where? Where is that place?" I was mad that I hadn't asked her, and I thought about turning around; but as I moved through the hallway, something else caught my eye, something that made me forget everything else.

Ava was talking to Mici. He was so fake—good looking, great personality, athletic, but no substance. I saw Ava say yes to him about something, but I couldn't make out what it was.

As I walked over to her, I thought about how beautiful she had become over these years. I thought about the nights we laughed at each other through the windows, especially if we didn't know the other was looking. Many times one of us had been doing something stupid, like talking to ourselves in the mirror, and the other would just watch and laugh when the other finally noticed.

As I approached them, Mici saw me coming and immediately said, "See ya." He gave me a stupid grin as he walked away.

I asked Ava, almost protectively, "What was the deal with that?"

"Nothing much," she replied almost casually. "He just asked me out."

I then laughed and said, "As if you would go out with him. I wish I could have seen his face when you told him no."

I noticed at that moment she had a little grin that shouted, "I am special," but I quickly took it away when I screamed, "WHAT?" I said it way too loud and then realized people were turning to see what was going on. Ava was a little startled as well, and I could tell as she said, "It's just a movie, stupid. And what do you care anyway? It's not like you and I are dating."

I regained my composure and quickly replied, "Yeah, you're right. It's just that he's a creep and I don't like him."

She quickly came back with, "Well, maybe I do, and you're not the one going on the date anyway, so what do you care?"

As she was walking away, she again looked back at me and said, "Collin, don't always judge a book by its cover. Sometimes people can surprise you."

She was leaving me, and I had to get the last word in, so I yelled out as she walked away, "You can if the cover is stupid looking." That was pathetic, I know, but it's all I had, and it did make her laugh.

As I got to the last class, I was dreading it and relieved all at the same time. I knew Monica would be there, and we had been going out for about two years, and I liked her a lot, even loved her a little I guess.

We had gone through way too much for such a short period of time. As I sat down, she looked at me and smiled. "We are still on for tomorrow, aren't we?" she asked.

"Absolutely," I said.

As we settled down, I couldn't help but think about Ava going out with Mici. She was right, though. Why should I care? She wasn't my girlfriend. Telling myself that however didn't matter though as it still bothered me.

As I was still simmering over their date, I felt my mind drifting back to Monica, and this time it wasn't a vision; it was reality.

I thought back to the night we went out and things got really heated in the car. It had been a perfect night, and she looked so hot. I remember touching her and how it made me feel. I wanted to just devour her in every way. In the middle of the most sensual moment, she whispered, "Do you think this is a good idea, Collin?"

Without a second to decide, I said, "Yes, doesn't it feel that way to you?"

It was an awesome night, but the month following was not. I remembered getting the phone call and the silence that followed. Monica told me she was late, and I asked for what.

She said, "No, doofus, I am late for my period."

My heart dropped, and I felt clammy, not knowing what to do. I said, "Can I come over?" She said yes and asked if I would pick up a pregnancy test to find out for sure.

I got one from the pharmacy, hoping I didn't see anybody I knew. As I checked out, the lady looked at my items—a pack of gum, a drink, and a pregnancy test. She then raised her eyebrows with a long sigh. "It's for my mom," I spoke up. I could tell she didn't believe me.

When I got to Monica's house, her mom gave me a hug and said, "Come on in, Collin. How are you, baby?"

She was so nice to me. She was a partier herself and was on her way out that night. Her husband had left her and Monica three years earlier for another woman, and it was obvious she was trying to act twenty in a forty-five-year-old body.

Monica was on the couch, and I sat down beside her. She laid her head on my shoulder and breathed a long sigh and said, "What are we going to do if I am pregnant?"

I just sat there. I didn't know and wasn't sure what to say, so I just said, "Maybe you're not." I handed her the test and nervously said, "I guess there is only one way to find out." She took the test and went into the bathroom. It seemed like hours as I waited in the living room.

As she walked toward me, I knew the answer before she ever said a word. Confusion and fear were painted on her as if written on her forehead; the blue positive symbol shined bright in that little white area, brighter than anything I had ever seen. We just sat there for minutes, not saying anything, and then she finally broke the silence, saying, "What do you want to do?"

I don't know. What do you want to do?" I said. All I could think about was telling my grandmother and the shame it was going to bring. I knew what I wanted her to do, but I didn't say it.

She said, "I want to finish high school and go to college."

In almost a whisper, I said, "Me too."

We didn't say it that night, but we had both made up our minds about what to do. In the weeks ahead, I got all the info and set everything up for an abortion.

I went with her that day and sat in the waiting room. I was so scared, not sure what to expect but glad I didn't hear anything from the back. The waiting room was very nice and pleasant. It was as if we were there for a physical. There were other guys there, but we didn't speak. We all knew what was happening, and none of us wanted to deal with the reality of it.

I was screaming on the inside, though, hating the situation I had put myself in. I wanted to hit myself, and I was angry at the circumstances, but never once did I think about the life that was ending just doors away behind the white, fresh walls of this waiting area.

As I continued screaming at my stupidity, mad at myself for getting into this, she came out, and we simply left, relieved that what we thought to be a burden was now no longer our concern.

I remembered the look of lifelessness on her face as I drove her home. And I realized we had lost something that day we could never get back, and the worst part was we did it for ourselves, for a life we thought we wanted. We sacrificed the life of one for the dreams of two.

We drove back to her house, and before she got out of the car, I looked at her and simply said, "I'm sorry."

The look on her face as she left me that day was one of both despair and relief. It was a look of sadness and loss and of failure more than anything. She said, "Don't worry about it, Collin. It was both of us, not just you." She then got out of the car and walked into her house.

I was quickly awakened from these memories with a resounding ring of the bell and a flash back to reality. I was happy the bell rang, as I didn't like to think about the deeds of my past. I quickly shook it off and decided I would rather think of the excitement of the future.

The next week went by quickly. Now that graduation was coming, I had so much to look forward to in the summer and the months to come: going to college, the bigger parties and the beautiful women, not to mention making money and having all this freedom without my grandmother looking over my shoulder. I was going to move out, and I could not wait. First things first, though. "First week at the beach" was in two weeks. I had been given money for graduation, and a bunch of friends and I got a room in Myrtle Beach, South Carolina. We had everything planned. We had already bought the drugs and the booze, and Monica and I had decided to go our separate ways, so now I didn't have a walking reminder of what we had done.

I was not really happy about the breakup, but it seemed to give us both a clean slate to forget everything and start fresh. It was kind of funny; the date she wanted to go on was to tell me she wanted to end our relationship. I cared about her, but it was a mutual decision. Both of us wanted to move on with our lives and leave the past in the past.

I wasn't sure what college I wanted to go to, but I figured it would have to be a tech school since I had not thought about anything other than learning a trade. My grades would be laughed at by a four-year institute anyway.

My grandma, Memaw we called her, didn't have much money, but she told me we would find a way to get me into school. She always said, "I will pray about it, and God will take care of it."

For me this prayer thing didn't work very well. It worked for her, but God and I were not so tight I guess. I didn't want to waste my time with God anyway. I mean, if He even existed, it sure wasn't a perfect world He made, so didn't that make Him not perfect? I think I really knew something had to have created this world, but if God was real, He didn't want anything to do with me. Anyway, I thought about taking the year off and getting an apartment with friends, working and just enjoying life for a while.

As I was packing the night before the beach trip, I looked out my window and saw Ava brushing her hair. I threw a penny at her window to get her attention and almost cracked the glass. It scared her a little, and she opened it up.

"What are doing, Goofy?" she said,

"Nothing, Cinderella," I replied quickly. "Where are you going all dressed up?"

"I am going on a date if you must know."

"With Mici, I guess?"

"Yes, with Mici. He has been really nice, and we are going to a drive-in." She looked down as if she wasn't sure she was doing the right thing in her mind.

"A drive-in? That's for making out."

"Maybe for you it is, but for us it's a movie and conversation."

"Listen, Ava, I just don't have a good feeling about Mici. He has always been a womanizer, and I should know."

"I appreciate it, Collin, but I will be fine. What are you packing for?"

"The beach! Ohhh yeah, ohhh yeah," I proclaimed with song, as I raised my hands in the air. She laughed at me when I yelled it out, and I started laughing as well.

I really liked Ava. I guess you could say she was my oldest friend, and I never had to act any different around her. She liked me for who I was, and that was pretty unique, especially since I didn't even like who I was.

As we ended the conversation, I closed my window and waved good-bye. I did say before we ended, "When I get back, let's go fishing at the pond." She said yes, and I was off.

We arrived at Myrtle Beach early the next day, and it was awesome. The sun was hot and the girls were too. We unloaded all of our stuff in the room and started to party. Everybody was there, and we started playing drinking games pretty early in the day.

Our plans were the same every day. We would start the day with a little food and then start drinking in the room. Then we would head to the beach. We would drink some more and usually try to rest a little before the night, though that didn't happen too often. When night came, it was no rules. There would be fights with ourselves and other partiers around us, people sneaking away to make out, people passing out, and of course someone would always go to jail.

The rush of all this was the freedom from all the rules life had given us. It was exciting ruling our own lives without anyone controlling any of us.

I realize now I had no control over anything around me at the time. The only control I had were the choices I made, and even then I was so consumed with getting high, drunk, and sleeping with girls I wasn't really in control. It was more like I was a slave to all of it. My addiction to those things made it impossible to choose anything other than those things. By the last day, I was broke and ready to go home.

The last night was the wildest one of all. We went to our friend Travis's room that night around 7:00 p.m. I went into the bathroom to take a peek into the mirror to make sure I looked okay. As I entered I saw two girls who were passed out in the bathtub. They had clothes on, but they had vomited on themselves, and the smell was horrible. I went out and said to Travis, "What's up with the girls in the bathroom? Are they dead?"

"No, stupid, they just couldn't handle the liquor," he replied.

We all sat around the table to start some drinking games but I couldn't help but think about Ava and her date with Mici. He had a football scholarship and didn't come to the beach. He surely would have been there if possible and would have been the most obnoxious one of the bunch. He would get drunk and be the first one to start a fight and mess up the night. I remember hating the fact that Ava would go out with him.

The beach trip finally ended. The drive back was the worst, as I realized I had to go back to what I had run to the beach to get away from: my life and the reality of the failure of it all!

Chapter 5

Matthew 7:16

As Ava got dressed, she stood in front of the mirror, looking at the dress her mother had bought her. It was red with straps coming over her shoulders. It wasn't revealing but was beautifully elegant. "Too much for a drive-in, but who cares?" Ava whispered to herself.

This was a special night for Ava, and she had every intention of enjoying it. She felt gorgeous and wanted to relish this moment as long as she could. It really didn't matter what she wore, though. She had blossomed over the last two years. She had filled out in all the right places, and the guys were all noticing.

As she sat on her bed putting on her earrings, she gazed out the window into Collin's window and into his room. The room was dark, but her memories of doing that for the past ten years were not. She had always thought Collin was cute, but it was the serenity she felt around him that she treasured the most.

Matthew 7:16

As she stared into the window, she could remember all Collin's little flaws. She laughed at his rebelliousness, as she knew it was for show, just as she knew he had a heart bigger than the moon. She knew more than anyone the hurt he felt from the absence of his parents, but it just made her care even more for him.

She finished curling her hair and put on just a touch of perfume as she heard the doorbell ring. She took one last peek into the mirror before leaving the bedroom, not realizing that after tonight her bedroom would never feel the same.

She walked down the stairs and into the living room. Mici was standing at the door. He was definitely handsome but in a rugged way, as if he were battle tested. He smiled as she opened the door to leave and stepped into the warm night.

As they walked to the car, Mici leaned close and whispered, "You look awesome, Ava. I'm really glad we're going out."

Ava smiled and thought for a moment before answering. Finally, she said, "Me too." She said it with just a hint of hesitation. It was not enough for Mici to even notice, but something just seemed off about him tonight. He was probably just nervous, she thought.

That's what people liked most about Ava and were even a little jealous of: her innocence and honesty. You always got the truth from her, whether it was good or bad. Most of the jealousy came from the girls who had already defiled themselves with another and resented her purity, secretly wanting theirs back, I believe. These attributes are hard to come by nowadays, and Mici knew it; he had plenty of experience with girls who had already been with others.

As they drove to get a bite before the movie, they stopped at a red light, and Mici leaned toward Ava again. He said, "I realize I have a reputation of being the jock and a little bullish, but I am not what everyone thinks."

Ava quickly replied, "You're into sports? I didn't know that. And why do you keep leaning into me every time you say something. Do you think I am deaf?"

Ava grinned, but Mici didn't find the humor in her words at first. For a moment Ava saw something in his eyes that scared her. He quickly realized this and jokingly said, "You're so funny, Ava." He started back off as the light turned green.

Of course in a weird sort of way her comment about him being a jock only fed his ego. He knew she was playing with him.

"I don't let my true feeling out about much," he continued, "but I want you to know I really like you."

"Thank you for that; thanks for the compliment."

After a long pause, Ava finally broke the silence again by saying, "I like you too. You know, that's really the reason I accepted your invitation. I wanted to find out who you are under that letterman's jacket."

As they ate at a small diner, Mici told a few jokes, and they both laughed. He finally looked down at his watch and realized they were going to be late for the movie if they didn't hurry. As they got up to leave, Mici said, "I need to use the bathroom first, so I will meet you at the car." He handed her the keys as he walked away.

Ava waited in the car quite a while, but when he finally came out the door, he sprang into the car, and they sped off quickly.

"What did you do, rob the place? Why are you in such a hurry now?"

"I'm not in a hurry, just excited to be with you, gorgeous."

He seemed way more relaxed as they drove to the movie and had an excitement about him that was not there earlier. She wasn't certain, but she thought she smelled a hint of alcohol on him, very faint, so faint as not to mention it yet. She was definitely going to keep her guard up regardless, though.

When they got to the drive-in, Mici parked away from the other cars—to have a little more privacy, he said. Looking back later at that moment, Ava realized what his real motives were for this. This was the third time Ava had started to feel a little unease, but she was not going to let that stop a so-far pretty good evening, so she decided to not raise any red flags. If something went wrong, she felt she could handle herself, and they were in a public place anyway. What's the worst that could happen? she thought to herself.

The trailers had started. The sun had set, and Mici asked if he could get Ava a drink and some popcorn. "Sure," Ava replied. Popcorn was one of her favorite snacks.

The movie had started by the time he returned, and they both began watching the movie in silence. As the movie progressed, Ava felt her eyes getting a little heavy, and she could definitely smell alcohol in the car now, much stronger than before. Ava finally looked at Mici and said, "Have you been drinking?"

"No way. It's probably just something in the air. Are you okay? You seem a little tired?"

She wasn't sure why she felt tired, but she didn't want to seem rude, so she slightly laid her head on the side of the headrest in a tilting fashion and gave a small yawn. She replied, "No, I am fine, just a little worn out, I guess."

As soon as she did this, two of Mici's friends walked by and waved as they continued on to their own car. Her eyes were growing even heavier now, and she wondered why she was so tired all of a sudden.

She dozed off for a split second and then woke back up to Mici slowly turning to her and saying, "How are you feeling? You okay?"

She smiled and said, "A little tired I guess, but I'm okay."

Mici slowly moved closer and kissed her softly on the cheek and then moved toward her lips. As he kissed her, Ava felt good at first, but as the kiss continued it became a little too heated, so she pulled her head back. He then started to kiss her neck, and she immediately said, "That's enough."

Mici acted as if she had said nothing, and this was when she realized something was terribly wrong. In that moment terror filled her veins, and helplessness surrounded the cells in every part of her body.

When she said, "That's enough," the words were in her head right, but they didn't come out right. They seemed slurred in a way, and she realized it, but she could not understand why it was happening.

She lifted her arm to push back, but it was as if it was in slow motion, almost as if she had had a stroke. She realized she was defenseless to anything that he was doing to her.

Mici then laid her down in the front seat and started to touch her everywhere. He had a look in his eyes far different from anything he had ever shown before, and he was locked in on her, his eyes devouring her entire body.

Fear again coursed through her system as if pumped, going faster and faster, but she could not react to anything.

"Please, no!" she finally screamed with all she had, but the movie was loud, and it was but a faint whisper in reality. Mici seemed unrelenting in his actions, like a crazed animal breathing erratically and moving his hands all over her in a force unlike anything she had ever felt.

The next thirty minutes in that car was Ava's worst nightmare coming true and was the last thing she thought would ever have happened. When Mici finished his assault, he left the car without saying a word and went to the restroom. Ava had tears rolling down her face, and terror encompassed her as she went in and out of consciousness. She was hurting everywhere and wanted to run, but it seemed as if her body just would not cooperate. She grabbed the door handle of the car to open it, but as soon as she did Mici jumped in and they drove away.

On the ride back, Mici kept saying he was sorry, over and over again like a broken record, as if Ava would accept it. She could smell the liquor on his sweat and breath now more than ever. It was so strong it made her want to vomit.

She wanted to vomit but couldn't. The fear, the smells, and the memory of what he had done all burned into her brain.

As he drove, she felt herself pass out. When she awoke, she was at her house. She could see the front door, and fear again paralyzed her as she wondered what he was going to do next.

Mici got out and carried her to the door. Her parents weren't home, and he knew this from the conversations they had had in the days before the date. He opened the front door and carried her to her room and laid her in her bed. It was the same bed into which her father and mother tucked her at night. It was the same bed where she read her Bible and the same bed that used to be a place of comfort. Now it was a place of horror. As he left the room, she looked at him as if her very life had been taken from her and said one simple thing: "Why? Why would you do this?"

He looked back with a glaze, and as he shut the door, he said, "I'm sorry. I couldn't help myself. You don't understand."

He closed the door, and Ava fell unconscious with her face covered in tears and the smell of Mici's sweat.

When I got back home from the beach two days later, I went straight to my room and passed out on the bed. I was so tired of partying, and my body hurt from getting no sleep. I must have slept for twelve hours. I finally woke up to rain pouring outside my window. As I woke, my stomach was growling from needing food and some real nutrition. As I looked out the window, I could see Ava kneeling in front of her bed, praying. I had seen this before, but this time she looked different. Maybe it was just me, but I felt something was wrong with her.

I couldn't help but go closer to the window to see what was up with her, but the rain was pouring, and it made it hard to see anything clearly. That is when it happened. The vision rushed into my head quickly. It was Ava getting ready for her date with Mici. It was strange because until this very day I had never had a vision of Ava. It was hard to take it all in. My head was pounding from being hungover anyway, and the pictures were rushing into my mind way too fast, so much so I had to grab hold of the headboard to keep from falling.

It started with her leaving with Mici and getting into the car as they drove off. I saw them finish eating, and I saw him go into the bathroom at the restaurant as she walked to the car.

As he was in the bathroom, I watched as he poured liquor down his throat like it was water. Next I saw him driving her to the movie, smiling at Ava as if he could not wait to get her alone. I saw them at the movie, as he went to get their drinks and popcorn. But on the way back to the car, he stopped on the side of the building and filled his cup with liquor and hers with some powder. At the moment I saw the powder I wanted to scream no, but I couldn't speak. I started to sweat as I saw all this, and my anger was growing from trying to take all of it in. I tried to pull away and come back, but it wouldn't let me. I didn't want to see anymore.

Next, I saw him give her the drink, and I saw every single detail afterward. I saw him take her in her weakness; I saw the entire nightmare, every loathsome event that took place. It was torture watching this movie that I didn't want to see.

I started to swing into the air as if I could hit something, as if I could hit him. How I wanted to so badly. I wanted to kill him. I was so angry I could feel my face tightening and turning red. My hands were turning white from squeezing my fist so tightly.

Again I tried to stop the vision; it was too much, too fast, and too heartbreaking, but I saw it to the end as he brought her home and staggered back to his car and left. I fell on my bed and screamed as loud as I could. I felt like he had taken something not only from Ava but from me as well. It was the purity of who she was and the innocence of her goodness as my friend. This was something that I loved about her, and I felt like what he had done to her he had done to me too.

I yelled again as my grandmother rushed in to see what was wrong. Ava must have heard me as well, as she had closed her blinds when I looked back to the window.

Memaw squawked, "What's wrong?"

"Nothing Memaw. I'm good, I just need you to leave me alone. Okay?"

"No, it's not okay," she barked back. "If you're going to act like a crazy man, I am going to question you."

I just sat there in disbelief at what had happened. Memaw finally broke my trance by telling me breakfast was ready. "If you want some, you better hurry before it gets cold; but please refrain from yelling and scaring me to death. Okay?" As she walked out, I heard her mumble, "I am too old for this."

I ate the breakfast but spent a lot of the time just staring at the food and thinking of the wonderfully horrific things I could do to Mici for what he had done. I knew I never liked Mici, but I didn't know he was capable of this.

One thing I knew for certain, though: I now hated him and I was going to find a way to get even, and that was a fact. I was going to think of something that would destroy his life if I could. I finished eating and got dressed. The rain was still pouring, but I had to see Ava, so I went over and dashed under her carport to ring the bell. Her mom came to the door with a halfhearted smile.

"Hey Ma'am. Is Ava home?"

"Yes, she is Collin, but she's not feeling very well, I think."

"It's okay, ma'am. She doesn't mind if it's me. I really need to talk to her."

"Okay, if you insist but please not too long. She is in her room, so go on up."

As I walked up the stairs, I gazed at all the pictures of smiling family members and pictures of Ava with that perfect silly happiness that everybody wanted but few had. It was like she had a secret happiness that you couldn't figure out.

I knocked on the door. "Ava, it's Collin. Are you okay?"

"No, not really. Can we talk later, Collin? I'm just not feeling well."

"I know," I said, and then I wondered what that sounded like since I had not seen her in a while. She knew I could not possibly know how she felt.

She opened the door and looked at me with a long stare, trying to decide what I meant by saying that. "What do you mean, you know? You know what?"

I backpedaled and lied. "Your mom told me." I was great at lying on the spot and not easily trapped. I could see a little relief fall over her as she assumed I didn't really know. I am sure she was in fear of Mici telling people what had happened—not the truth, of course, just that he had gotten with her.

I could tell she was full of shame, and I wondered why she felt shame for something he did. I felt only anger, and I wanted to get even with Mici so badly it was coming out in my attitude.

Ava just lay back down on her bed, and silence filled the room. I finally broke the deadness in the air by saying, "Are you okay?"

She looked at me for the longest time and said, "Have you ever had someone take something from you that wasn't theirs—something you really loved, something that defined who you were in a way?"

"Not really, but it sounds like that would suck."

"It does, Collin, and I don't know how to get it back."

At that moment, for the first time in all the years that I knew Ava, I saw that the secret happiness of hers had disappeared. I could think of only one thing to say, and I am not even sure where it came from. I looked at her and said, "You define who you are, not anyone else. No one can take anything from you if you don't let them. No one can take your identity from you, no matter what else they take. Your identity must be given, and that takes surrender, and you have always been a fighter."

"Nothing is as precious as that, Ava, and people can't take that from you, regardless of what they do," I continued. "That's why people love you so much. That's why people want what you have."

With those words, she broke and started to cry. It was more like a sob, a release of sorts. I wasn't sure whether I should leave or just sit there. As she cried, I just listened to the sound of her sobbing, and it caused me to have emotions I had never felt. It was too much. I couldn't hold back and finally I blurted it out: "I know, Ava. I know what happened."

I almost put my hand over my mouth. I didn't know why I said it, but I couldn't help myself. It was too much.

She immediately stopped, as if a switch had been turned off, and looked at me with a gaze. I wasn't sure what was going to come next. It was a combination of anger, fear, strength, and weakness all in one.

"What do you mean, you know?" she pierced back at me.

"Wait, Ava, you don't understand. There is something I have not told you are anyone else for that matter. It's going to take a minute, so please calm down so I can explain."

"You explain, and make it quick," she shouted back at me.

For the next hour, I told Ava everything. I told her all of it, all that I could remember anyway, from the time I was little to the death of my father. I even told her of the teachers and students at school I knew things about. After I finished, she looked at me in disbelief, and all she could say was, "Are you for real, Collin? How is this possible?"

"I don't know, but you're the only one who knows, and I want to keep it that way."

We sat in silence, absorbing everything that had just been discussed. It was at that moment in her fear and weakness, in her tears and beauty, that I realized something. I realized I had never before felt so attracted to another person like this. I realized without saying it at that very moment. I acknowledged to myself that I loved her, and I think she felt the same for me, but neither of us spoke a word about it. Before I left I hugged her for what seemed a year, and at that moment a bond was established between her heart and mine. It was a bond that I would later realize would last a lifetime.

That day, in a way I had never felt before, I had peace. I had peace when I was with her from that moment forward, and it was a peace I didn't want to ever go away. Before I left I told her I wanted to talk to her more about Mici, what he did, and what we were going to do about it. She didn't share my anger, but we agreed to meet the next day at the pond and discuss it.

As angry as I was at Mici for what he had done to Ava, I left her with a feeling of hope, a feeling of fulfillment, and in the weirdest way, an excitement about what the future may hold for us.

The next morning was bright, and the sun streaked down on my head through the window. I woke up wondering if everything had been a dream but realized it was all too real. My anger for Mici was growing to an epic point, and it was consuming all my thoughts. I imagined so many ways of torturing him. I wanted him to die for what he did, but I realized that would be too easy of an escape. What I really wanted for him was to suffer and suffer greatly, and I wanted to be the one to cause it.

The doorbell rang; it was Ava, coming to get me so we could go for a walk to the neighborhood pond. Memaw answered the door and hugged Ava as she came in. She loved Ava like no other girl I had ever been friends with. When Ava would come over, they would sit on the couch and talk about God and Jesus and whatever girly things came up. They always made me laugh when I saw them sitting there discussing things and playing with each other's hair, always complimenting each other's appearance. I walked into the living room and saw them embracing as If they had just had one of those talks. My grandmother seemed concerned but smiled it off. As we walked out the door, Memaw stopped us and said, "Collin, I want to do something before you leave, and I need you to come here for just a minute."

"We gotta go, Memaw," I barked back. "We ain't got time for this."

Ava pushed me on the arm and said, "Listen to her, Collin, you dummy."

"Okay, whatever. Let's get it done, okay?"

Memaw grabbed Ava's hand and mine at the same time, and Ava grabbed mine. I realized it was about to be prayer time, and it made me uncomfortable to say the least—almost laughable—as I didn't see much value in praying.

Memaw rarely included me in her prayer sessions, but I believe I was the topic of most of her prayers. As I closed my eyes, her voice seemed as if it was lifted up directly to heaven, and my laughable moment became very surreal. She prayed the following: "Father, I know You have plans for these two, and I pray You will watch over their every step. Jesus, please strengthen them above their understanding, above their ability, and above their means. God, please hold Ava in Your arms. (At this point I could feel Ava's weakness and tears, as she wept through the rest of the prayer.) Keep her focused on You Lord, and shield her from any harm that may come her way. God, I pray for Collin that You would use his abilities to serve You and Your will in this life."

Matthew 7:16

I was about to pull away, as it was just too much, when she ended by saying, "We are yours, Father, Your children. All that happens is under Your watch, and we trust in You."

As we left for the park, there was one thing I was certain of after all that had happened with Ava. I would never trust in a God who would or could let that happen. Yet I believed Ava could and still did.

Chapter 6
Jerimiah 29:11

As we sat by the pond with poles in hand, the sun was bright and the air was humid. There was just enough breeze to make it enjoyable. We didn't speak much at first, and finally Ava broke the silence by asking me a question. "So what's next?" she said, almost emotionless.

What a question to ask with all that had happened. I had no idea what to say. I had no answers, just hate. I just said, "I don't know." After a while I finally added, "Clarify your question. Do you mean what's next for you or for us?"

She paused at my response and then looked straight through my eyes. It was like she could see my soul, and it made me feel naked. My heart was melting as I waited for her response. I really couldn't believe I even had these emotions for her, especially sense I had never realized them before.

She finally replied, "I was talking about what I should do next about what happened with Mici, but the other one is a good question too."

"You know what, Ava? I don't even like the sound his name makes when you say it. From now on let's refer to him as the turd or the idiot, something more fitting for who he is. Back to the question at hand I continued, I don't really know what the best thing is to do next, but I do know what's next for turd man, and that's my fist in his face and him going to jail for what he did to you. I could really see myself killing him, Ava, and having no problem doing it.

"He took something from you that can't be given back with any, 'I'm sorry' or 'I'll do better' crap. Aren't you mad at him for what he did? Don't you want him to pay for this? You seem to have peace, and I don't understand it. I think you need to go to the police and tell them exactly what he did. They'll drag his tail in for questioning at least, and when they prove what he did to you, and he is in prison, I hope they do the same thing to him."

"Stop, Collin," she said, as she placed her hands on my face. It was scary feeling this way about her, but as her hands were on my face her touch alone seemed to bring me to a place of peace.

"Collin, I don't want that. I don't want that to happen to anyone, not even him. Yes, I am angry, and I am confused, but I don't want to get even. I just want peace from this."

As I sat there realizing I was making things worse, not better, I looked at Ava with humility in my voice and just said, "I am sorry. I need to just shut up and be here for you."

She put her arm over my shoulder and said, "Yes, that's sounds great." I laughed at the fact she agreed with me shutting up, and I finally got a giggle out of her too. It was good to see her smile again, even if for just a second.

After a few minutes, Ava turned to me with the smile gone and in a very serious tone, said, "I am scared, Collin, to report this because it's so humiliating. But I know this: Mici needs to be stopped before he does it to someone else. I wonder how many others he has done this to, how many girls just like me."

This got my temper going for another round, so I stood up on the banks of the water with the pole still in my hand, gripping it as if I could crush it. I raised the pole back as if I were some warrior ready for battle, reaching my hand out to make my proclamation to Mici's end at my hands. "I can guarantee you this," I yelled out: "he won't do this again around here." Just as the words were coming out of my mouth, I turned to take a step, and the mud under my feet at the edge of the lake glided my right foot into the air. The next thing I felt was the cool water hitting my back and the laughter of Ava roaring through the air.

The lake was deep and cold, and I was in shock when it happened. I let the pole go as I felt the water go above my head. I came up as if I were a cat and somebody had thrown me into a pool. I climbed back onto the bank at the continuous sound of hysterical laughter from Ava. It was so loud and contagious, all the anger and frustration I had felt before was quickly replaced with embarrassment and humility. Ava laughed so hard she snorted, and then all I could do was laugh with her. The rest of the day was just us, alone and at least peace for a little while.

As I dried out that day, I asked her, "So are you going to the cops, and what about your parents?"

"I don't know yet what to do, Collin. I need a little time."

"No you don't, Ava. That's the wrong idea. You need to tell your parents immediately, and he needs to be arrested."

"You're right, I guess. I'll tell them tonight. Will you come with me?"

The word "no way" screamed through my mind, but the word "yes" came out of my mouth. Her eyes had a way of making me do this more times than not.

That night was hard for everyone. I just sat there and listened as her dad hugged her and her mom cried. I wasn't sure what to do. At the end of the discussion, they decided they were going to call the police the next day and press charges.

Truthfully, I wanted to just go over to Mici's house and take care of it myself. At the time, however, it seemed like it would only make things worse, and I had another idea anyway. I knew where he would be the next night, and I was going to be there and have my own revenge.

As the conversation ended with here parents, Ava's dad did the craziest thing. He prayed. He prayed for truth, peace, resolution, and tolerance, and to end it he actually prayed for Mici's soul. He was furious I could tell but I guess the prayer for him was a way of not doing what he wanted to do. It made me angry to hear those words because I didn't want Mici to be saved by God or anyone. I wanted him to be punished. I considered Ava's father weak for doing this, but it was strange, for he was not a weak man at all. He was angry, and I could tell. I could see in his eyes he wanted revenge just as I did, but he controlled it, and that was something I could not and would not do.

The next morning I saw the police car over at Ava's, so I stayed away. It seemed like they stayed all day, and other cars came in and out as well. I wanted to see her before I left to go out, but I couldn't get to her.

I took off that evening. I was ready to teach Mici boy a lesson about life and payback. I arrived at the Beacon Drive-in around 6:30 and parked. This was a place where you could get a burger and sit outside and just hang with friends. I parked and noticed Mici and a few of his friends, as well as a girl he was with, laughing and cutting up. He had no reason to worry about me since he didn't know I knew anything.

I got out and walked toward the car. I was just going to hang out a while and try to bait him into a fight, but then I decided the best thing to do was just walk up and knock him out cold and let the chips fall where they may. I couldn't wait to do it. I was almost giddy. I was actually excited about it, and for a minute I almost forgot why I was doing it. Maybe it wasn't just about vindicating Ava but about vindicating the world from jerks like him.

As I set out with my pace in long strides, a vision started and my mind was pulling me away. I fought it harder than ever but to no avail. I was on a mission, and this so-called gift was slowing me down.

My mind took me to a large, well-groomed house. I saw Mici looking at his dad's porn tapes in a large basement room. His dad walked in on him, and I saw them arguing. Mici fell to the ground as his dad struck him across the face. I saw him beat Mici with a belt until he couldn't move and was curled into a ball. Then I saw another image of Mici sitting at his computer engrossed in porn; it was like he was imprisoned by it. He didn't look happy or appear to be enjoying it; he looked addicted. He was clicking on page after page with his eyes focused on every detail. He seemed tired, but he was still relentless, as if he were on some quest that had no end.

As I came to myself, I realized I was almost to him, and I wasn't sure what to do. I wanted to punch him, but I also felt a little pity for him at the same time. I was conflicted. I just wanted to hurt him, not feel sorry for him. But as I approached him, I was still committed to going through with it. Just then I saw the police car come from the side, and everyone straightened up.

A rather large officer jumped out and asked Mici his name. He had one hand on his gun, and we all just froze as he approached.

When Mici acknowledged who he was, the officer said, "You are under arrest."

"For what?" Mici barked back.

"For rape son, for rape."

Everyone gasped, and Mici looked at his newest girl and said, "Call my dad, and tell him what happened."

That night and the days to come our community was full of rumors and gossip. The lies and stories grew, and before long it seemed like Ava was the criminal, not Mici. Isn't it strange how money and popularity have a way of doing this, regardless of the truth?

For Ava most of this time was spent with meetings filled with lawyers and police. She had to go over every detail of that night, over and over again. Many times she would get sick and could no longer go on, but they never stopped grilling her. Almost every day she had to live that nightmare over again—how he touched her, what it felt like, every action he did. If it were not for her faith, which I didn't like or understand, I believe she would have just given up. Closer to the court date, I was asked to come in for a deposition and was asked a ton of questions myself about that day and the conversation Ava and I had.

Ava's lawyer asked me more about our relationship than he did about what she had told me in her room that night. It seemed as if he was building his case to show what kind of person she was instead of finding out about who Mici, the rapist, was. I finally said, "What are you doing? Ava is the purist, most innocent person I know, and

Mici is a freaking criminal. Why are you trying to defend her? She's is the one who got raped, not him."

I was so enraged by the time Mici's lawyer started to ask questions I wanted to hit him in the mouth before he ever said a word, just for being his lawyer. I imagined reaching across the table and smacking him in the face just to shut him up. I didn't, though. I tried to answer his questions as briefly as I could. I didn't want to give him anything to help his case.

Two of the questions he asked me seemed strange at the time, but later I realized what he was doing. First, he asked, "Did Ava like Mici before that date?"

I had to say yes, but then I added, "It was only because he was lying to her."

"That's enough, Mr. Keith. Just answer the questions," the lawyer scolded me.

The second strange question was, "Did you ever see them being romantic?"

As soon as he said that, I remembered that day in the hall that Mici was very close to her at her locker and they were discussing their upcoming date. It made me nauseous. I told him that was the closet I had ever seen them, and that was the last question before I was told I could leave.

From the time the incident happened to the trial date was only two months. I believe it happened so quickly because Mici's lawyer was the best in the state and he pulled some strings. The trial went on for four days, but the last day was the worst. Ava was on the stand, and the jurors were obviously irritated at having to be in the court. Mici's lawyer and Ava's attorney had been going at it pretty hard and had already interviewed Mici as well as the friends who had seen them at the drive-in that night. It was Ava's turn next, and the prosecutor went first.

Ava again had to go over every detail. She told the truth from beginning to end, everything he did to her and what it was like afterward. She told the jurors the kind of person she was and what this had done to her. I believe if at that moment they had deliberated Mici would have been convicted on the spot, but that's not the way our court system works.

When it was Mici's lawyer's turn, he started in on Ava, and he seemed to be given a lot of latitude to do so. He asked very personal questions, like whether she had ever thought romantically about Mici or any other boys and what those thoughts were. He asked if she had ever been touched in certain places before. Finally, the prosecutor objected, and the judge agreed.

The attorney's closing argument was that no one knew the whole truth about that night and without the whole truth, the jury could not find Mici guilty. The jury was out for eight hours, and the next morning they came out to give the verdict. The lead juror stood and was asked if a verdict had been made, and the man lowered his eyes as if he were ashamed to say it but then uttered, "Yes, your honor. We find the defendant not guilty!"

I could have blown up at that very moment. I felt my head pounding and my heart beating rapidly. I wanted to protest, but my focus was turned to Ava. She had her arms around her mom, and both of them were sobbing. I then focused on Mici and his dad hugging him. At that very moment, Mici looked at me, and our eyes met. I remember thinking, If he smiles at me, it is on right now in this courtroom. He didn't smile, though; he only had a look of despair, as if he were lost in the woods all alone. I thought he would be relieved, but he wasn't. He looked as if he thought they had found him guilty, or as if he had found himself guilty.

That night I was lying in my bed, still trying to figure out how this could have happened when I heard the gravel hit my window. I opened it up to see Ava wanting my attention. I opened my window and asked if she was okay.

"Not really, but I want to talk to you tomorrow if you have time. Can you come over in the morning?"

"Yeah of course."

"Okay, I gotta go. See ya tomorrow," she said as she closed the window.

The next morning I woke up to my grandmother asking me why there was a moving truck at Ava's house.

"I don't know, but I intend to find out," I said. I threw on some clothes and sluggishly walked over to her house to see what was up. As I entered the front room, I saw her mom packing clothes and her dad and a couple of men moving the couch. Her mom told me

Ava was in her room, so I proceeded in that direction and tapped on the door.

"Hey, Ava, it's Collin. Can I come in?" As I entered I could see almost everything was packed up. "What's up with this?" I felt like breaking down because I knew the answer, but I was more mad than hurt.

"Sit down here, Collin, and let's talk for a minute."

As we sat she told me that as a family they had decided they needed to move away from this place and start new. Her father had gotten a job in Florida, and it was even more money. She said they would be leaving the next day.

With everything going on, she needed a fresh start and was going to attend tech school when they got down there and maybe become a social worker. I tried to convince her to go to college with me, but after a while, I knew it was no use. Finally, I said I understood. Before I left the room that day, Ava looked at me without a blink. Her stare pierced my soul as her hands touched my face again.

She then slowly gave me the most wonderful kiss I had ever felt in my life. It wasn't sexual or meant as a come-on. It was intimate, warm, and caring. Afterward, she said, "I will miss you so much." She thanked me for being her friend and sticking by her through all of this.

My life changed forever after that day and that kiss. It was going to take some time to realize it, but I never before and never after felt that way about another soul.

Ava was gone the next day, and within the next week Mici had taken off to college early in the summer. He was going somewhere in Texas, and I was glad he was gone. I still wanted revenge though. Some way, somehow I would make him pay for what he did. I knew why he left so early too. Most people knew in their hearts he was guilty, at least we all did, and his scholarship was in jeopardy through the whole incident. His dad pushed him out as soon as the trial ended, and it was like nothing had ever happened.

I was just mad at life in general. I was mad Ava was gone, I was mad Mici got away with it, and most of all I was mad at God, if there even was one. I was more than ever ready to live my life to the fullest. I had one more month before I started college, and I was ready to get on with this new life.

I had to go to the technical college first because of my grades, but the good news was I had found two roommates and we had our place lined up. I was so ready to start this new, better life and put the old behind, all of it. It was not until the night we moved in and got our place that I realized, as usual, what I thought would be magnificent ended up being significantly less than that. That first night we had the party to beat all parties, but in the mist of all that drinking and fighting and laughing, I had never felt more alone. All I could think of was Ava and all we had shared. I wondered where she was. I missed my friend.

Chapter 7

1 Samual 16:7

College was pretty tough; I guess it was payback for all the brain cells I killed with the drugs and booze in high school, my first semester I had to even take a few dummy classes before I could take real credit courses. The consequences of doing so poorly in high school and never taking my college SAT were biting me in the butt.

By the end of my first semester, both my roommates were flunking almost everything, and I was struggling just to stay awake. My friends however had their parents' money, but I had to get a job and the partying every night was getting old fast. We rarely cleaned, and the place was getting nastier every day. The family of rats didn't seem to mind, but it would freak me out when one would run across the floor at night when I was watching TV.

It is sad but we actually gave them names and would joke about them if one ran out during a party. The girls always freaked out, but

I found a great use for them. I would set up a trap and catch one live and then keep it in a shoe box until I needed it. When I met a girl I liked and didn't want to bring her to the house, I would rent a really nice hotel room. When we were finished partying for the night and she left, I would then let the rat out in the bathroom and go get the manager. They always made a big fuss and gave me my money back for the room and sometimes even a complimentary night for the future. It is amazing what scams you can come up with when you put your mind to it. We may have acted below the morality norm, but as trashy as this sounds; our standards were set by driving nice cars and wearing expensive clothes.

After some time of this lifestyle, I had to start putting plans together to get my own place, but my job as transporter in a local hospital didn't pay much. This job was a hundred jobs in one. I worked in the x-ray department, and they made us do everything it seemed for the least amount of money.

My main job was to take patients from their rooms down to x-ray and then back up, but the x-ray techs at this place had me doing all kinds of other stuff. If a patient puked, call Collin. If they soiled themselves, call Collin. I got used to the spills, the messes, and the smells, but the worst part was the sickness everywhere.

We had AIDS patients who came down, and I always knew which ones they were by their soft hair. I'm not sure why they had soft hair, whether it was the medicine or the disease, but I always wore a mask and double-gloved my hands because that was some scary looking stuff. The open wounds and lesions they had all over their faces and hands were disgusting. I didn't have much sympathy for them either. I figured most of them were gay or drug addicts. I didn't have much room to talk about drugs since I had my own addictions to deal with, but they got the disease and I didn't, and for some reason I thought this made me better than them.

Yes, I used drugs but not the bad ones like heroin or anything that involved needles. That was for junkies, and I worked for a living; I wasn't some junkie. AIDS was for those who should have known better. I was better than that, at least in my mind anyway.

This opinion, however, completely changed one fateful night when I was working second shift. I had not had any visions in a long time, and I was thinking maybe I had finally stopped having them. I didn't know if I should be disappointed or relieved. I had really gotten used to them in a way. I have to admit my special ability to see these things made me feel special in some ways; it was the only special thing about me I guess.

What I finally realized later was that the less I cared about people, the fewer visions I had. I was so busy partying, going to school, and working, caring about people was not an important concern. This particular night, however, I had been called to go to the AIDS ward and bring a guy down for an x-ray of his abdomen. I tried to get Brenda, the other transporter, to do it, but she said no way and started laughing at me. It was my turn anyway, she cackled back at me. Brenda was funny and looked like Uma Thurman in a way, so it was hard to give her too much crap, so I double-gloved and headed to the floor.

The thought of going to this floor wasn't all bad because there were some hotty nurses there, so at least the trip was not a total waste. I stopped on the way to talk to a particularly smoking one. She was so fine, and I had asked her out several times. She liked me, I could tell, but she knew who I was. She knew what I was about, so she played hard to get, and I played right along.

I had this way about me. I'm not bragging; I'm just saying I was like a chameleon with the ladies. Whatever they liked, I liked; whatever game they played, I was all in. In fact, that they even played any game at all with me meant I was half way home already. We danced the same old dance as we spoke, and every time I got a little bit closer to the grand prize. After a few minutes of this, I realized I was behind and I went into room 404 to get Mr. Fredrick Brown.

It's funny in life how some things just stay with you forever. This was one of those things. That name and that room number are burned into my brain and for good reason.

I approached the door and immediately noticed that it looked different from the others. It had cards all over it, and I remember thinking, don't they always put those on the inside of the door, not the outside. Later I realized the inside was already filled. I knocked on the door, and I heard his voice crack as he said to come in. I entered this deathly dark room and turned on one small light since both lights would have been way too bright. I wished I had left them both off after what I saw, but it was too late.

The smell was horrible, and the sight of Mr. Brown was even worse. He had that same soft hair and lesions all over his face. I felt sick just looking at him, but I had to smile and hide it for his sake and mine. I pushed the stretcher beside his bed to pull him over and asked if he was okay. I didn't really care, and I didn't wait for him to answer. I just told him why I was there. It was a stupid question anyway. He obviously was not okay, but I had to be polite, and I was just making conversation and trying to get through this ordeal. However, His answer to my question stopped me in my tracks. I expected a long reply enumerating all his ailments and problems. To my surprise I got just the opposite.

He looked at me with a passion in his eyes that I had rarely seen, only from my grandmother and Ava. He said, "Yes sir, how are you doing?"

I didn't know what to say. I mean he was the one dying from a nasty disease caused by his own actions, and he asked me if I was okay. Finally, after an awkward moment of silence, I said, "I am great." I paused before pulling him over and then said, "I am good; thanks for asking." After another pause, I said, "Well, to be honest, Mr. Brown, I guess I am just okay."

Why am I telling this guy anything? What is wrong with me? I must be tired, I thought. As I pulled him over to the stretcher, he said, he saw my name badge and said, "Well, Collin, I am sorry, but it sounds like you're 'okay' is more of a 'not so okay.'"

"I'm just tired," I said, "and I need to get some sleep, I guess." As I got him situated on the stretcher, I could tell the pain he was in was horrible. I guess you do suffer consequences for your mistakes, I thought. It scared me a little thinking this way since I had been making a few mistakes myself lately and didn't want to think about the results. As we rolled down the hall, I could hear him talking to himself, and then I realized he was praying, and not only praying but praying for me. That's just great. This was really awkward now. I started to speed up a little as I realized this AIDS was going to his brain. I did realize something, though. I had a diseased AIDS guy with a short time to live praying for *me*. I had definitely hit a new low.

As I pushed the elevator button, I saw the light slowly coming down to our floor, and then it happened. I had not felt this in a long while, but it was rushing in like a train. I could feel the blood pumping in my head, and the vision was coming. I tried to focus and stop it, but it was no use. As it started I saw that it was this same man, Mr. Brown, with his family. It looked like it was around Christmas time. They were praying over a big meal, and his whole family was there. I saw his oldest son, who looked to be around fourteen, and his younger two daughters smiling and laughing. They all looked like something out of a Norman Rockwell painting. I saw his wife lean over and kiss him and whisper, "I love you," as he laughed along with his girls. His wife then opened the refrigerator and said something to him. Mr. Brown quickly got up, grabbed his keys, and left the room with another kiss to his wife. How happy they looked, almost too happy. I had never seen that much joy shared between people or among a whole family.

Then I saw him driving to the store and pulling out into an intersection; the driver coming down the road in a large truck was asleep at the wheel and went right through the intersection and the red light. I saw the impact as pieces of his car were obliterated by the massiveness of this truck. The ambulance came quickly and then the surgery. The family were all together in the waiting room. The vision quickly turned to the doctor in the surgery room, who said he needed four pints of AB positive blood. They brought it in and gave it to him through his IV.

Next, I saw the recovery period and him at the doctor's office, with the doctor coming into the room to let him know the blood he had been given was infected and they had had no way of knowing it. I saw his wife sobbing, and then he grabbed her hand with the calmest of intent. He was as calm about all this as if they had told him he had a cold. He turned to his wife and said, "It's going to be all right, baby." Then I saw him by himself on his knees, crying and praying to God for his family and friends. What was even worse was I saw him tell God he loved Him. In the last part of the vision, I saw him receiving treatments, and I witnessed the results of the disease coming on.

I came back as I heard the bell ding to let me onto the elevator. I couldn't breathe after seeing all this, and I hated myself for judging him the way I did. I quickly swiped my eyes as I fought back these emotions. As we went down in the elevator, I couldn't say a word. It was almost as if he knew that I knew all this.

He finally said, "Collin, thank you for the ride. Will you be taking me back up?"

"Yes," I replied.

He quickly responded, "Good, because I want to talk to you some more."

I realized I said yes out of guilt more than anything, but as crazy as it sounds, I thing I really wanted to listen to him more than anything, I guess because I knew he genuinely cared for me and I had not felt that from anyone in a long while.

When the exam was done, I got him back to his room and into his bed, and he asked if I could sit with him for a moment. I told him I would. I was still feeling a little guilty; now that I knew the truth of what had put him in this place.

As I sat there that night, I really just listened to him. Among the bells of his IV pump going off, and the wind blowing against the window, and the occasional paging of someone, I just listened.

I had never really met anyone like him before. He was passionate about his family and his life. I was actually a little jealous, wishing I had a dad who loved me that much. He talked about his wife and the strength God had given her through his sickness. He was completely at peace with where he was, and I just didn't understand how. But I remember wanting it. I wanted the peace he had even through the pain. Before I left he said something I will never forget as long as I live. He said, "Collin, this world has a lot of curve balls, but if you got the right swing, you can hit every one." We laughed as if we had known each other for much longer than we did, but in some strange way I felt he did know me. It was almost as if he could discern everything about me, and there were only a few times I felt that from anyone else, and never from a man. It made me think of the only other person I could think of who had ever made me feel that way before, Ava, of course.

I caught myself drifting off to thoughts of her, and then realized I had been sitting with Mr. Brown for almost an hour. I told him I needed to leave, and that's when he asked if I would come see him the next day. "Absolutely," I replied. I had enjoyed myself, and believe it or not, it made me feel good doing something for someone else. I had not felt good about anything in a long time, and it was a refreshing emotion. I actually felt alive again for the first time in so very long. For a moment I even forgot about his sickness, and he was just another person.

The next evening at my dinner break, I hurried up to Fredrick's room but on the way stopped off at the front desk to see if Tasha was working. She was so fine, and I think she liked the fact I was attracted to her. The problem was she had a husband. I didn't care too much. If he was not making her happy, then maybe I could. It was almost a challenge to see if I could win her from him. I didn't want a relationship, mind you, just the physical attraction was enough. As

1 Samual 16:7

I approached she had her back to me, and I whispered, "Hey, pretty thing." She slowly turned around and smiled a half-smile. It was not what I expected. I asked what was wrong, and she said one of her patients had taken a turn for the worse. I asked who it was, and to my shock she said it was Mr. Brown. She said the medicine was not helping as much, and the doctors said he probably had only a few days left.

I realized then something had changed about Tasha. Before she was always responding to my come-ons, but something was different now. I asked if she wanted to hook up later, and she said no. She went on to say, "I really have been doing a lot of thinking lately, and I need to make some changes in my life, Collin. I have not been doing the things I should, and I have decided to change the direction I'm going in."

I realized things were not the same, so I cut her off. That was good, I guess. I quickly told her I better get going because I wanted to say hello to Fredrick before I went back to work.

As soon as I said that, she looked at me with her eyes filling with tears and said, "You really should listen to him, Collin. He helped me realize what I needed to do with my life."

This was getting way too deep, so I ended the conversation by saying, "I hope you feel better. I'll see you later." I really didn't care if she felt better; I just realized I wanted to leave.

As I opened the door to Fredrick's room, I could see his family with him. I tried to just say hello and leave, but he insisted I come in so he could introduce everyone to me. He had a way of making me feel almost important. This was not something I felt very often, and I really didn't know how to handle it. As I sat there with his family around him, I could see the life draining from his eyes. I tried not to stare too long, but it was almost mesmerizing to see someone fading away as he was. His young sons were bickering a little, and his daughter was on the bed with him. His wife was straightening up the room, and I could tell she was keeping busy to deal with the stress.

In the midst of this, Fredrick looked at me and said something that still resounds in my head almost every day now. I can't stop remembering that moment, with death, arguing, and busyness all around him, when he looked at me and said, "Collin, you see I am the luckiest man in the world."

It took a minute for his words to sink in, and I still couldn't process it all. I knew he didn't say it because he was trying to find a better way of looking at life; he said it because he really believed it was true. He was truly happy. As soon as he spoke the words, his wife began to cry a little. She leaned over the bed and laid her head on him, as if he were comforting her and not the other way around. I guess he was.

I was just about to leave when Nurse Barbara walked in. She was a bitter person and should not have been working on this floor. As usual, she was all business, and in her rough nunnery voice, she said, "Okay, visiting is over. Mr. Brown needs his rest, and I need to do my job."

I wanted to smack her in the face and say, "Shut up, stupid, and leave us alone," but of course I didn't. The kids didn't like the idea of leaving, and neither did I. His daughter started to tear up as she hugged him. It was clear the tension was getting worse.

Just as the tension was getting to a breaking point, all of a sudden from Fredrick's bed we heard the sound of a ripped fart. It wasn't a quiet one; it was an intentionally forced loud one that seemed to shake the covers a little. As the nurse and everyone stopped and silence fell in the room, everyone turned to the direction of the sound. We all looked at Fredrick in astonishment.

Then, as if he were as shocked as all of us, Fredrick said, "Ms. Barbara, that was unnecessary, wasn't it? Boys tell Ms. Barbara we say 'excuse me' when we do that."

At that moment it was if the seas had parted. The boys began to laugh uncontrollably, and it was contagious. Fredrick's daughter began to giggle, which led to her snorting a little.

Fredrick looked at me and said, "That's my favorite sound by the way—the giggle, that is definitely my favorite sound."

Even his wife began to fight back the laugh and could only say, "Fredrick, really?"

Barbara, however, did not know what to do. She wanted to laugh herself, I believe, but didn't let herself. She gasped and said, "Mr. Brown, that was you, as if we didn't all know it." Her chubby cheeks began to turn red, which made us all laugh even harder. Realizing she was the butt of this joke and the laughter was not ending, the nurse said, "Mr. Brown, I will be back in a minute, so please try to refrain yourself."

If I had to guess, I believe she had to compose herself, and that is why she left. She probably went outside to laugh herself—or cry. After the laughter died down and the tension was broken, the kisses were given, and they all left, saying, "I will see you tomorrow" and "We love you."

The last to leave was his daughter, who leaned over and whispered something in his ear before she took off. As soon as she whispered it, tears began to swell in Fredrick's eyes. When his daughter was gone, he turned to me and said, "You know what she just said to me, Collin?"

I didn't want to know. I was about to cry, as the emotions were running high anyway. But I said, "What?"

"She said I was her hero and she loved me. Collin, that's why I am the luckiest man in the world."

As the tears streamed down my face, Fredrick hugged me as if he were my dad, and the tears became even worse. I could not remember ever being hugged like that by a man, and it wasn't awkward; it was needed.

As he let me go, he said, "Listen, Collin, I want you to read this." He handed me a note and said, "I ask one thing of you: after you read it, come see me tomorrow if you have time."

I said I would, and I left, wiping my face, not sure of how or why all of this had just happened.

1 Samual 16:7

When work was done that night, I went home. For once, it was quiet. The roommates were gone. I lay in my bed, and as I opened the note, the one thing that came to my mind was Ava. I realized I missed her more than I ever thought I would. Isn't that the way it is, though? We realize the things we love the most when we are separated from them. I wondered if she was okay. Then I began to read.

Collin,

Thank you so much for the time you have spent with me. I am so glad I got to meet and get to know you. Please know you are in my prayers every day and night. I know this may sound a little strange to you, but God has told me he has a plan for your life, and it starts with this scripture: "Ye have not chosen me, but I have chosen you, and ordained you, that ye should go and bring forth fruit, and that your fruit should remain: that whatsoever ye shall ask of the Father in my name, he may give it you" (John 15:16).

> In light of this, Collin, I am so very excited for you. I realize your mind is reeling from this, and I am sure you have a lot of doubt and misunderstanding of what I am telling you. But remember that God's calling on someone is not something to be put aside. Your questions about who God is will be answered in time, but know this, son: He is always there for you, and He says he will never leave you nor forsake you.

This is a lot to take in, and I am sure you may have a lot of questions. Some I can answer, and some I can't, but please ask, regardless.

Finally, Collin, I realize you have not lived a perfect life; none of us has. God is not calling you to live a perfect life but to have a perfect life living in you. Please continue to come by, and know this above all: I love you regardless of your past or present; my love is unconditional.

As I read the letter, I couldn't believe it. I had so many emotions running through my head. God calling me? Was Fredrick a nut job? I mean, really, if God knows everything, He knew my deeds, the abortion, the drugs, and the sex, and with all of that baggage I was quite sure there were better candidates than me.

What really got me was not the believing-in-God part. Even I was not so foolish to think a world and universe as complex as ours could have come from nothing. It was that he said he loved me and didn't care about my past and that he enjoyed my being around. Something inside me wanted that from a man, and at the same time I was angry at my father for not being there for me, and I hated him for that. The hate almost won out as I put the letter down. But as I sat there that night, I found myself actually praying for the first time ever. It was not the prayer of a child but an actual conversation I wanted to have with God. I said, "God if You're real and this stuff is real, I need You

1 Samual 16:7

to show me. Show me You love me and You will never leave me. Show me You forgive me for all my deeds. More than anything, I just want some peace."

I closed my eyes and drifted off to sleep thinking one thing: Did He really choose me? Could it even be possible?

CHAPTER 8

Romans 6:18

The next morning I woke up early and actually felt good for the first time in a very long while. I had energy and a demeanor I had really never felt before or at least in so log I couldn't remember it.

I hurriedly jumped into the shower and dressed for work. I was actually excited to see Fredrick, more than anything just to say thanks. I grabbed my phone as I left and saw that I had a missed call.

As I sat in the car and waited for it to warm up, I checked the message. It was from Ava. I was really excited when I saw her name, and I fumbled the phone out of my hands, and it fell to the floorboard. I am such an idiot sometimes, I thought. Why am I so excited to hear a voice mail?

The message was brief, but it was Ava saying all was well in Florida and she hoped we could talk soon. She said she missed me and would be thinking of me and praying for me always. She mentioned she had a lot going on and would talk to me later. She really just wanted to say hello.

Today was starting out as a great day, and I didn't want it to end. I got to work and handled a few patients. All the time, I was looking for a way to get to Fredrick's floor and take a break. The day rushed by, and before I knew it the day was over. I clocked out and went up to Fredrick's room to say hello. As I approached the door, I noticed it was cracked, and I could hear people talking inside. I know I shouldn't have done it, but I listened in. I could hear the seriousness in the doctor's voice as he told Fredrick and his wife he could give Fredrick pain medicine, but the end of his life was near and he didn't know what else he could do to help.

I stepped way back as they ended and saw the doctor and the wife leave. I softly knocked on the door as I heard Fredrick say, "Come in, Collin." I walked into the room and asked him how he knew I was at the door. He said, "I just knew, buddy. I just knew."

He looked horrible. His face was caving in, and his hair was all gone now. He had so many IVs poking in him, and his breathing was getting shorter. His voice crackled as he spoke. "Did you hear what the doctor was saying?"

I wanted to lie and say no, but for some reason I couldn't lie to Fredrick. I didn't want to lie to him. I guess I knew he wouldn't judge me and I felt a peace around him. "Yes, I did," I said.

He just smiled and breathed a sigh of release. All I could say was, "I am sorry."

He again surprised me with his response: "What are you sorry for, Collin? I have had a beautiful life. I am saved and have peace in Christ. I have been blessed with a loving family that loves me more than I love myself. I have had friends I didn't deserve and been a part of God's calling. I have seen God work in so many lives, and now I get to be with Him. Do you hear me? I get to be with Him forever."

"I am not sorry and neither should you," he continued. "Sorry is about regret, and I have only one regret: I wish I had trusted Him even more in my life than I did. Death is at everybody's door; it's just a matter of when it is going to knock. I am blessed that I got time before it knocked on my door.

"You won't understand this now, but believe it or not, death is really just the start of the real life forever. We see death as an end, but God made it into a beginning."

"I want to believe it, Fredrick," I responded as I cut him off. "I just don't know how."

"Take my hand, Collin. Salvation is not something you just believe in; it is surrendering. It is surrendering to God. It is surrendering your sin, yourself, and all you have become. It is as if you are committing suicide to self, though not to your body but your soul. If you want a life of rest and peace, you must give up the life you have made and turn it over to the One who gave His life for you."

I could feel something in my soul at that very moment. I held his hand tighter and said again, "I want to, but I don't know how. I don't have anything to give Him."

"You give Him yourself, just as you are, Collin, nothing else."

"He doesn't want me," I blurted back.

"That's a lie. Don't believe that. He does want you. You know your sins, right? You know all the things you have done that you loved but are bad and you knew you shouldn't have done them. All the regrets—those are the things He wants you to give."

At that moment—and I wasn't even sure where it came from—I said, "If I do, I know He will not love me anymore."

Fredrick looked at me as tears ran down both our faces. After a moment of silence, he finally whispered, "He already knows, Collin. He already knows, and He loves you anyway. He died for you, for this."

I began to feel courage for the first time, courage to say yes in spite of my doubt. "Yes, I will give Him everything, Fredrick—all of it."

"Let's pray, then, and make this thing for real."

I closed my eyes, and it seemed as if we had traveled to another place, a place of safety and rest, a place of peace and solitude.

"This is your time, Collin, your prayer."

I opened my mouth, and the words came, unrehearsed and from my heart. "God, I have done a lot of things I know I shouldn't have and I'm still doing them. I'm sorry, but I can't take them back. I don't know how You can forgive me, but I know I want You to. Please, God, let me be free of who I am. I need Your help. I know You sent your Son to take my place, and I accept that. I am unworthy of it, but I will take it."

As I spoke these words, I felt a great release. I felt lighter. It was a rest I had never felt before; it was like chains had fallen off. A tidal wave of guilt, shame, anger, and pride all rolled off of me in one gigantic passing. I felt freedom, relief, joy, and sadness all at the same time. I realized I was hugging Fredrick now, but it felt more like I was hugging God Himself. I didn't want it to ever end.

Finally, Fredrick said, "Collin, it's done, buddy. You are His now, and nothing can ever change that. I smiled as I sat back down in my chair. Fredrick just sat there with a dazed look of victory. It was like he had been a part of defeating someone in battle and he was relishing the triumph. We sat there for minutes without saying anything. I wanted to ask him a million things, but it wasn't the time. We just shared the rest and the quietness.

After a while, I realized he had fallen asleep, and I had to go anyway. I left the room unsure about all that had happened, but I knew something had changed in me and I wanted to know more about it.

That night when I got home, the guys were all home having a party. The girls were there as well, and they were all drinking. The smell of cigarettes and pot filled the air. As I walked in the door, a roar of yelps came forth. Everybody was glad to see me. I wanted to tell someone what had happened, but I knew no one wanted to hear it. At that very moment for the first time, I felt separated from them.

It felt strange. I had known them all for so long. I had spent so much time with them and even had sex with some of the girls, but I didn't feel a part of them anymore. It felt great really, but at the same time, I felt sorrow for them; it was worry more than anything. I knew they were having fun, but I realized now it was fun only because it was an escape, a break from reality. I told them, "I gotta take a shower, guys." I laughed it off and went into the bathroom. I knew from that point I would not be at that house much longer. I felt I was destined for another place.

When I finished changing, I went back out, and things were dying down a little. I walked into the living room and sat down on the couch beside Amy. She was one of the girls I knew from school. No one else was in the room with us, and she didn't say anything at first. She just gave me a little smile, and we both stared at the TV. She reached for her beer, and I noticed her hand had a small cut on it. I started to ask about it, but before I could, a vision poured into my brain.

I saw Amy getting dressed that night as she came down the stairs in her house. Her dad and mom were obviously angry at what she had on and scolded her for being so revealing. Amy became angry and pushed her way through as her friends, my friends, were blowing the horn for her. Her mom grabbed her arm, and they started to struggle. Amy pulled away, and her hand hit the corner of the door. "I hate you" were the last words that came from her mouth before the door slammed shut.

I came back and found her looking at me inquisitively. "Are you drunk, Collin? What are you doing?"

I sat there for a second and then finally spoke: "No, just thinking."

She leaned back on the couch and said, "Me too." Then she repeated the words. I thought it strange that she said it twice.

"Not as much fun as it used to be, is it?" she said. The next thing I knew she leaned over and started kissing me softly on my neck. I was surprised. I really wasn't expecting this or looking for it. I certainly would have been before.

It took a second to take it in. She backed away and looked at me and then said something that surprised me even more. As she kissed me on my neck, she whispered, "Do you want to be with me tonight?"

I gently turned toward her. I could not think of what to say at first, but then the words came. "Amy, you are beautiful, and anyone would be lucky to be with you, but I can't. I just can't."

I felt bad for her because this was the way she showed she liked me—and others I am sure. As tempting as it was for me to take her up on the offer; something inside of me stirred up compassion for her, not lust.

This was a very strange, new feeling. Before I already would have been in my room with her because it would be about me, but now I just wanted to help her in some way. I felt bad for her; she just seemed so empty.

"What's the problem? Is it me?"

I quickly responded, "No, it's definitely me; I have been going through some changes of the heart, Amy. We have been friends a long time, and I don't want to use you that way."

She looked into my eyes, not sure what to think. Then her eyes widened, and she said, "You love someone; you're in love with someone, aren't you?"

She was right. I was in love, but I wasn't sure at that second who it was I loved more, God or Ava. I guess now I realize it was both. She nailed it that night, though. I was in love. I was in love with what God had done to me. I was free for the first time in my life, free from who I used to be, free from hating anyone, even Mici for the time being, free from my past, present, and future. I guess that is the best way I can describe it; I was free from the world.

I also realized that I loved someone else more than I loved myself; it was a rushing feeling of desire and passion, caring, pain, and longing, a wonderment of sorts. This love was for Ava, and while I was sitting there holding another girl's hand, I told myself Ava was the one, and I was going to go to her as soon as I could.

Amy and I just sat there. We didn't talk much after that, but I did bring up her family situation a little, and we talked about why it was the way it was. I think for the first time in my life I actually helped someone else without it being all about me. Instead of avoiding trying to avoid my discernment ability, I actually used it to help someone.

As I drifted off to sleep that night, I realized one thing: this was the beginning of a whole new life for me, and I was excited about living it. Now everything was new, and the old stuff had just passed away.

I woke up the next morning feeling great. I jumped up, got into the shower, dressed, and headed to work one last day before I was off for two weeks on a needed vacation. Half of it I wanted, and the other half I had to take off because my employer was cutting back hours on us.

As I left the house that day, I saw my friends passed out from the drunken fest the night before, and I couldn't help but again feel bad for them. It was that same sorrow I spoke about. When did I start caring so much about others? I wondered. I realized as I closed the door to my car that I never wanted that life again. This was the first time I actually breathed deep and enjoyed it.

As soon as lunch came at work, I went to see Fredrick, but as I approached the room, I knew what had happened. I walked into the room, and the bed was neatly made. All was wiped down, and like so many times before, the room was empty.

I went to the front desk, knowing the answer I would get, but I needed to ask anyway. Tasha stood there as I approached, and I tapped her on the shoulder to get her attention. When she turned around, I could tell. She didn't need to say a word. I just shook my head.

"Was it peaceful?" I asked, "Before it happened, I mean."

A big smile crossed her face, and "Absolutely" came from her lips.

I turned to leave, knowing I had nothing left at this place or in this town except my grandmother. I just wanted to bolt, and I did just that. As I was leaving, I turned to Tasha one last time and said, "Hey, by the way, girl, I am sorry for everything. I realize now who I was, and I am not very proud of it."

Tasha looked at me with the same peace I felt and said, "You too, huh?" "Absolutely" came from her lips again, as she embraced me and we parted ways.

I worked the rest of the day and then went to Memaw's house to fill her in on everything. When my grandmother was finally done doting over me, I went home and packed as fast as I could. I emptied my bank account and decided I would surprise Ava instead of calling first.

Chapter 9

Psalm 90:14

Driving from Columbia, South Carolina, to Clearwater, Florida, is about six and a half hours, but it feels like six and half days. The long stretch of I-95 was full of trucks and vacation goers along with a handful of speed traps. I had plenty of time to talk to myself on the way, and it all seemed to make sense the more I thought about it.

Everything seemed so much clearer now. My thoughts were more specific, not jumping from one to another, and I spent time pondering each one. Before salvation, I was in a constant jumbled state, going from one thought to another, trying to figure out what my next move would be but never focusing clearly on any given one. Now it seemed everything was more transparent.

I guess it was also the lack of drugs and alcohol in my system; that would make sense too. But I knew in my heart that more than anything the real reason for this new clarity had to be my salvation.

I was so ready to get to where Ava was but scared to death at the same time. What if Ava didn't feel the same as I did? What if she had somebody else? I felt like an idiot already, but I realized there was something else driving me. This something drove me not to care about these matters but to go through with this quest, regardless of the outcome ahead.

When I arrived at her address, I drove quickly by her yard at first. I just wanted to see what I was getting into. I looked at the small yard and noticed her dad's car was in the driveway. It had been almost two years since Ava had left South Carolina, and I wondered how she had changed. I circled the end of the cul-de-sac and headed back toward the house. I parked in front of the neighbor's house so Ava would not see me coming. As I approached the front yard, I noticed a little yapping dog running to and from the door, trying to let them and everybody else on the street know I was there. I wanted to kick it but realized that probably would not be the best entrance I could make.

As I approached the door, I could feel my heart pounding out of my chest. My mouth was dry, and I suddenly realized I was more of an idiot than I ever imagined. But I didn't stop; I just kept moving toward the door. I had forgotten everything I was going to say to her.

I was such a mess I started hoping if I rang the doorbell and no one came, I might get a "do-over" in some way and come back later. As I rang the bell, I thought the world could hear it. It was like the Tower of London clock going off. I turned to look for any sign of life as the bell rang on. That no doubt had to be the loudest doorbell known to man. It was also the longest I ever heard. Finally, I heard the dreaded footsteps coming.

This was it, and I did not know what to do. When the woman came to the door with a baby on her hip, I realized I had the wrong house, and a sudden relief fell over me. She was a young Hispanic lady who had a wonderful smile. As soon as she opened the door, I apologized for coming to the wrong place, and she quickly said it was okay. "Who you are looking for, Maybe I can help," she added in broken English. When I said Ava and gave her family's last name, the woman smiled even bigger and said, "You're at right place, senor. Come on in."

Automatically I went straight back on freak-out mode as I walked in and sat down on the couch. The young woman said, "Please hold one moment, and I will get her." She went through the kitchen, but as she went she put the toddler in a playpen in another room. I could see the small child sitting in the little playpen chewing on a rubber toy. I was mystified by the child as it looked back at me. It was as if it were a forty-year-old in a little body sizing me up. It was a beautiful baby with curly hair, but for the life of me I couldn't tell if it was a boy or a girl. Whatever it was, I thought it looked a little bit like its mom, who had come to the door.

When Ava turned the corner, she had an inquisitive look as she tried to determine who was there for her. When she recognized me, she just stood there without saying anything. It was very awkward, and I felt embarrassed for a moment. Then, finally, I said, "Hey, it's me, Collin."

At that moment she leaped over the couch, ran over to me, jumped into my arms, and wrapped her legs around me as if she were a small child. She wasn't, of course, and we both tumbled back on the other side of the sectional sofa. She hugged me so hard I could feel myself losing my breath a little, and then she finally released me. She sat up and then sat down beside me and glared into my eyes. "I have missed you so much," she said.

I felt the warmth come from her smile, as if it were a blanket wrapped around me. She looked really happy, and I was glad.

"What are you doing here?" she shouted at me.

I really didn't know what to say. "Can we go get a bite and catch up, and I will explain," I said.

She gladly accepted, and we were off. As we were leaving, Ava waived to the lady, "Bye LeLe (short for Louisa). See ya in a little while, okay?"

LeLe through her hand up and said, "Go ahead and have fun. I will see you soon, Senorita."

We drove to a little burger joint just down the road and sat down after ordering. We just looked at each other for a while. It was awkward, but in a weird way it just seemed right; in fact, it seemed perfect. I hadn't felt this way about anyone before, and I was not going to hide from it any longer. Just as she started to say, "I need to tell you something, Collin," I blurted out, "You know I came for you,

Ava. I came for you. Did I just repeat myself? I am so stupid. What I meant to say is I came here because I want to be with you. Not like be with you, be with you, but be around you." Oh shoot, I thought, this is not working out like I thought. I was so embarrassed I finally just shut up to see what she would say.

Silence fell over our little area, as others stopped to listen. Ava never budged and never took her eyes from me. What seemed about two years went by, and she finally leaned over the table and put her hands on the sides of my face and kissed me. It was not just a kiss but a kiss that made my toes curl. The blood in my heart pumped so hard I thought it would explode. She stopped the kiss, as I think I would have kissed her forever. She leaned back just an inch and said with a smile of embarrassment, "Well, it's about time, dummy. I wondered how long it would take you." She sat back in her chair and continued, "I have missed you so much, and I have been praying for this day for a long time, Collin."

As we talked for what seemed like hours, I told her all about Fredrick and about giving my life to Christ. For that short time that day, it felt like we were all alone on this planet. Before I knew it, two hours had really passed. Ava looked down at her watch and said, "Oh no, we better get back."

"Why? You got somewhere to be?" I asked.

Again, silence fell over the conversation. Then she spoke.

"Collin, it's not just me anymore. There is someone else, and things are different for me now."

My heart sunk. I knew it was too good to be true. Was she dating someone else? Did I wait too long? Why did she say she was waiting for me? I waited to let her finish, but I really just wanted to leave.

"I have missed you, Collin, and I am so glad you came here to see me, but there's something you should know."

"I am sure I already know. What's his name?" I asked.

"It's Michael."

"Is he nice?" I asked as if I really cared.

"More than nice Collin, he is wonderful. He is everything I ever hoped for."

That's not what I wanted to hear. Her words were like pouring alcohol on an open wound; they were stinging more and more as she talked. I started to think how I could I talk her into splitting up with him, for I just knew I was the one she should be with.

My mind raced. "What is he like?" I asked and then immediately regretted asking it, as it was too painful. She spent the next ten minutes telling me how great he was, and every accolade seemed to make me more nauseated. I know I seemed disinterested because I was broken, but I tried to be polite. Finally, I asked if they were planning to get married. Then, again, silence fell.

She cocked her head and said, "Collin, are we talking about the same thing? Michael is my son, Collin, not my boyfriend."

"What?" I blurted out as everyone turned to look again. "How did that happen? I mean I know how it happened, but when? Where? Not where—but just tell me the story, and I'll shut up."

"There is no story, Collin. Michael is from Mici."

As she said those words, everything clicked, and I apologized for being so stupid. After they had moved to Florida, she found out she was pregnant and after much prayer she realized it wasn't Michael's fault his dad had raped her. She couldn't just take his life.

"I just couldn't," she said. "He is such a blessing to me, Collin. You just don't know. I want you to meet him when we get back."

Before we left the restaurant, she took my hands and looked at me again. "Collin, now that you know, do you still want to be with me?"

I looked at her beautiful eyes and soft smile and without hesitation said, "I have wanted you my whole life, Ava. I just didn't know it."

She kissed me again, and just like before my toes curled. But this time I manned up and leaned in for even a deeper embrace.

When we pulled back up to the house, LeLe was waiting at the door. She handed off Michael and hugged Ava's neck. She looked over at me as she was walking out. I think it was my butt she looked at, and then she said something to Ava in Spanish that made Ava laugh as the door closed behind.

We went back into the house and for the next couple of hours we were lost again in conversation. We talked as she gave Michael a bath and fed him and then as she laid him down.

She asked me as she laid him down for bed if I would read them the *Little Bunny Foo Foo* story, the one where you hold your hand up and make the finger figure as you tell the story. It is more like a song. The bunny keeps scooping up the field mice and bopping them on the head. At the end of the story, there is a moral: "Hare today, Goon tomorrow." I realized that moment, in that simple story, God was telling me to embrace today for tomorrow is not a given.

When Ava's parents came home, we all had dinner and laughed. It just felt like a family, the family I had never had. As the night grew late, I said, "I better go," and Ava went to check on Michael before walking me out. Before Ava returned, her dad looked at me and with a resounding voice said, "Collin, what took you so long, son?"

I just smiled and shrugged my shoulders. "I guess God wanted me to know Him first," I said. He liked my answer, I believe.

When Ava came down, her dad and I were laughing, and her mom was crying over the story I had been telling them about my salvation. Ava was confused.

"Just come on, Ava; it will take too long." We walked out the door, but before I got into my car, Ava put both hands on my face again. I so loved it when she did that. She looked deep into my eyes, and I was lost in hers. We slowly kissed again; it was always the first kiss over and over again. I knew when I left that night I had found the only woman I could share my soul with. Finally, I felt at home.

Over the next few months, I got a job at a school as a maintenance guy, and we were making plans to marry. Everything was going great. We had even found a church close by and were going on Sundays. What I loved even more, though, was the Wednesday night small group we had. As a new believer, I was asking lots of questions. I wanted to learn everything I could. I guess you could say I was all in.

We married in the late summer and got an apartment. I loved those two so much—almost too much. I was scared it was too good to be true. I had everything, I thought. Ava and I were passionate for one another, and not too long after the marriage, she was pregnant again.

Michael was getting bigger by the day. One day I bought him a scooter, and he loved it so much I started calling him Scooter. He seemed to like it pretty well. It just seemed to click, and before I knew it everyone was calling him Scooter.

I loved life like never before. I never thought it could be like this. It seemed like it would be this way forever. I am glad that at the time I didn't know what lay ahead. If I had known, it would have taken the joy out of where I was.

What lay ahead began to happen when I got the call on a Friday night at about eight o'clock. The first words were, "Is this Mr. Collin Keith?"

"Yes!"

"Sir, your grandmother has had a car accident, and she is in critical condition."

I hung up the phone, and my heart sank. I started to panic, but Ava quickly suggested we take a minute to pray and then get ready to travel back.

Psalm 90:14

Ava was awesome in so many ways, but what really amazed me was her prayer life. When she prayed, it seemed God was right beside us. Sometimes He even seemed too close for me.

As usual, praying did put things into perspective, and I was able to focus instead of freak out.

We packed the car and left Michael with Ava's parents and headed toward Columbia. I tore the road up, and Ava finally told me we would make it and to chill out. She said we didn't want to be in the same situation my grandmother was in.

When we arrived at the hospital, the ER doctor let me into the room. Memaw's body seemed battered, bruised, and lifeless. She had a tube going down her throat, and the ventilator was keeping her alive. The doctor came in and said exactly the opposite of what I wanted to hear.

"Mr. Keith, your grandmother has received fatal contusions to her head and neck and is on life support. Are you the closet relative?"

"Yes."

"Well, sir, we need to discuss some tough choices very shortly."

After I told Ava what was said, we spent some time praying and talking to my grandmother. I had the sense she was not coming back from this.

"Ava, I have got to get some air, and the police have to get some information from me, so I am going to walk outside. Will you stay with her, please?"

"Yes," she replied with a kiss to my cheek.

The policeman filled me in on the accident. He told me it looked like my grandmother had swerved into the oncoming traffic and was hit by the truck, which threw her car into a side ravine. He said the car was totaled, but the driver of the truck was not hurt badly. However, he was irate about her coming over into his lane. After a few more questions, the officer left to fill out the forms, and I sat there in the cold dark trying to take in all of this.

As I was standing there, I saw a man being wheeled out of the emergency room accompanied by a woman who apparently was his wife and some other family members. He was yelling about something, and I couldn't help but listen in to the conversation. The woman was asking, "Where were you going? I thought you were at work."

The man shouted back, "I don't know. I'm hurt, and that old lady almost killed me; so leave me alone."

I could tell the woman was not satisfied with the answer and continued to ask more questions. Suddenly I realized he was the man who was involved in the accident with my grandmother. The officer approached him and also began to ask questions, as the others stepped aside. The policeman asked him if he had been drinking or on drugs. He asked where he had been and where he was going.

Finally, the man yelled back, "I don't remember, so quit asking me. All I know is that woman came into my lane and I hit her. That's it!"

As soon as the words came out of his mouth, I could feel my mind taking me off. I saw the man coming out of a hotel room and a woman kissing him, as if to say good-bye. He got into his truck and headed down a curvy and dim road. He lit a cigarette and took a deep drag of satisfaction. Just then as he was reminiscing over his evening, he dropped his lighter in the floorboard. Aggravated at this, he reached for the lighter and in the process knocked over his coffee, spilling it in the floorboard.

Now he was really beside himself. With the music blaring, he sped even faster through the night. When he approached what seemed to be a straightaway, he reached down to pick his lighter up, trying to keep his eyes on the road at the same time. The curve came from nowhere, and as he rounded the first of it, he looked up only to see he was heading straight for a car. The car reacted by going into his lane to miss him, but almost simultaneously he jerked the truck back to do the same thing. He hit the side of the car, knocking it into the ravine, and down it went, tumbling as it reached its final resting place. As the smoke filled the air, he stopped to see how bad it really was. The adrenaline rushed to his head, pounding like a drum, one beat at a time. He suddenly realized he was bleeding, and he felt the sting running down his neck from the impact. As he got out of his truck and looked at the other vehicle, he could see my grandmother lying across the seats. More headlights appeared and then stopped. A man yelled that he had called the police.

"Is everyone okay in your truck?"

"Yes," the man responded.

As his questioner headed down to help my grandmother, the driver of the truck rushed back to his vehicle and took out what looked like a small liquor bottle and threw it into the woods as far as he could. He then sat down and put his hands over his face as he realized what he had caused. When the police and rescue team finally arrived, they asked him what had happened, and he told them my grandmother had come onto his side of the road. He tried to avoid her, he said, but he couldn't.

As I came back to reality, realizing what he had done, I wanted to break his neck for real. I was just waiting to get to him. As soon as the officer left, I went up to him, and the first thing I did was smack the cigarette from his lips.

His eyes widened, and I began my inquisition. That was my grandmother you did that to. His eyes got even wider, and after the shock of my statement, he immediately shouted, "She came over into my lane."

I cut him off. "I know everything—the real truth. Do you understand me? I know the truth. I saw the woman who was not your wife. I saw the bottle you threw out, and I saw the accident."

Now he began stammering, trying to find another way out. He asked how I knew this.

"It doesn't matter how," I said, "but you're going to tell the truth to everyone, and it's going to be now. If you don't, I will for you." I had never been so assertive in my life, especially after being saved, but this night the warrior in me came out.

The man immediately began to tear up and sob as if he were two years old. I was still angry, but I also felt compassion for him for some reason—not much but enough to listen to him.

He said he had been seeing another woman but did not want his family to know because he loved his kids and didn't want to lose them. He said he needed help and he was sorry. I told him to get his wife together with the officer, and we would do this together. I told him, "I won't say anything; I will let it be from you."

As we sat in that cold, white room at the hospital that night and the man confessed to everything, my wife and I could only feel sadness for him and his situation. At first, his wife grew cold to him, but by the end I could tell she loved him. As he spoke the truth, it not only confirmed what she knew already in her heart, but it also stirred up her compassion for him. The officer rewrote the incident report and told the man he would have to press charges, but he also told him his confession would serve him well. The policeman said he would do what he could for him.

The truth was as the officer stated. I had this man's future in my hands now. I had to make two important decisions that night; one was to help a man I didn't want to help and the other was to allow the doctors to take my grandmother off life support. I stayed at my grandmother's house that night after making both of those decisions, and as much as I didn't want to do either one, I chose to do both—to help and to let go.

Chapter 10
John 14:15

The years following the death of Memaw were filled with the joys and trials any family might experience. We had our second child and named him Spencer. I remember when he was born and the doctor laid him in my arms. I looked into his dark, brown eyes and dark, brown curly hair and immediately turned to my wife and said with the sweetest voice I had, "Baby, is there something you want to tell me? This child does not look like either of us." It was a joke, of course, and not timed too well, I must say, but in my mind I did wonder how I could have been part of such a beautiful creation.

There are two things I hope to never forget from Spencer's birth. The first is the realization that I can truly love someone more than myself—so much so that I would give my life for that person. The second thing I realized as I looked at my child is how God looks at me as His child.

As I sat there in that little room holding my child while my wife was sleeping, the Holy Spirit spoke to me almost as if I could hear the words audibly, "I love you this much and even more." I thought how impossible it seemed that anyone could love me more than I loved this child. Then I remembered studying in Sunday school that Jesus loved us when we were yet His enemies, so much so that He gave His life for us, even before we accepted Him as our Savior.

Just as I was basking in this revelation, Scooter, who had been so quiet this whole time, finally spoke up and said, "Daddy, do you still love me?" The question floored me; I looked into his sad little eyes and could see he was waiting for the worst.

I will never forget what I did, and it was one of my best moments as a dad. I got up and laid Spencer in the little bed, and I told Scooter to climb up on my lap. There were so many emotions running through my brain it was hard to speak. I looked him in the eyes and said, "Son, I love you so much I can't even tell you how much. You are so special to your mom and me, and nothing could ever replace the love we have for you, not Spencer or anyone else."

As relief came across his face and he hugged me, I just accepted how much I really did love him, knowing I was not his biological dad but feeling just as much as if I were. I thanked God for that moment, and as I picked up Spencer again, I realized my wife had been watching and listening through this whole incident and had tears in her eyes. She pulled my sleeve down and kissed me on the forehead. "Thank you for loving us, and thank you for coming for me," she said.

As much as my life seemed complete, it was just beginning a new chapter, a chapter I wasn't prepared for. Memaw left her house to us, and we moved to Columbia. We started going to an awesome church close to the house, and Pastor Mike was more than helpful in making us feel wanted.

The church was growing rapidly, and Pastor Mike asked if we would start having small group discussions at our house on Thursdays. It seemed like a good idea, and soon the group was getting larger each week. Mike had been encouraging many of us to follow the Spirit in teaching others. As a leader he loved to push people to serve God in any way they could. I think he knew we were capable of much more than we thought, and I now understand that the only way to show our full appreciation for what Christ has done for us is by serving others.

I had read the Bible through since my salvation, and I had been working with Mike a lot, mostly asking him a ton of questions. I wasn't like some of the other Christians I knew, who just accepted everything and smiled. I wanted answers. I was not questioning God out of doubt as I knew He had saved me and it was real, I was asking more like a young dad asks questions of his father.

Why is there evil? How did the world begin? What is heaven like? What is hell like? Why does God allow evil? Why do godly people suffer? What does God want me to do with my life? There were so many questions, and I was like a starving child with a hunger

I had never had before. I wanted to know these things. I wanted to know everything.

It was a newness of my nature I realize now, but at the time I was like the kid in the proverbial candy store. Pastor Mike would tell me, "Collin, remember to remain steady, but don't let the fire burn out. Ask God for these answers, and He promises He will give them in His time, not yours. Remember, sometimes He realizes we are not ready for the answers yet, and He gives us time to get ready for them."

I didn't like waiting, but he was right. I began to pray for answers, and as God revealed them through His Spirit and His Word, I would share them with others. When I shared these things with others, I would get lost in myself and not realize I had been going on longer than expected. But no one seemed to care, or maybe it was just that I didn't care. I had to start making sure it wasn't always me talking, so I consciously allowed others to express their thoughts. Still, it always ended with me closing the topic out.

The other issue I had to deal with was my discernment. I would see what was going on in people's lives. I never told them I actually saw these things, but I would try to direct our conversations to those things I knew they were dealing with personally. It was like playing poker and seeing everyone's cards.

Even Henry, the man involved in the accident that killed my grandmother, had been coming to church and the small groups with his wife, and the two were eating it up. Henry had given his heart to Christ, and their marriage was blossoming more every day.

Ava was awesome through this and always seemed to say just the right thing at the right time. I would see her glow as the kids would be playing at the table while we adults were all sitting around encouraging one another in the Word. I really believed she was living her dream.

By the end of the following year, the church family was growing and the small group had reached the capacity in our home. We weren't sure what to do other than meet at the church. The following week Mike asked me to come in to discuss something; he wouldn't tell me what it was about, just that he wanted to wait until we met to tell me.

I showed up at the church around nine on the day of our meeting and went to Mike's office, where I found myself alone. His secretary told me to go ahead and have a seat, so I went in and waited. It's weird sitting in a pastor's office. It feels like the principal's office in elementary school. I guess it's because a good pastor should have authority in your life. He had family pictures all over his desk and walls. It was a very warm environment, but I was still wondering why he was so secretive about this meeting.

I heard Mike coming down the hall talking to someone, and as they both entered the room, I realized this meeting was going to be more than just Mike and me.

The gentleman who appeared with Mike was a normal-sized man, but he had the most genuine presence of peace I had ever seen in someone. He introduced himself as Ken Russell and said he was a professor at a college outside of Los Angeles. I was really clueless

John 14:15

as to what this was about, so I just listened. As I did, I remembered seeing this guy somewhere; I just couldn't put my finger on it.

Mike opened the conversation, saying, "Collin, you know I have enjoyed our friendship over the last couple of years. I appreciate your dedication not only to this church but also to the individuals in it. I have seen you grow so much, especially this past year, and I wanted to bring in Dr. Russell to discuss something with you."

I was shocked since I never expected this, but I continued to just listen.

"Collin, Dr. Russell is one of the foremost Christian apologetics professors in the world, and I had him come here to see you for himself."

As soon as he said this, I realized who Dr. Russell was. I had been reading one of his books on defending Christianity. Now when it all came together, I was even more uncomfortable. I had had an interest in apologetics from the start. I just didn't know it was called that. Almost from the time I got saved, I would write down the questions I had about my new life in Christ. They were questions people just didn't seem to answer, like why God allows the innocent to experience evil and suffering. I had even had the idea of writing a book addressing each of these questions and naming it *Truth*, but that was just a pipe dream. I didn't feel confident enough in myself for that yet.

As Mike continued, he told me he and Dr. Russell had gone to school together and had remained friends through the years. He had been telling Dr. Russell about the growth in the small groups and the impact I was having on individuals in our church. He even mentioned that I had the ability, or gift, he called discernment.

That was the first time I had really heard that term for the gift I had: *discernment*. I didn't know what to say to all this and the professor must have thought I was an idiot because I was just sitting there taking all of this in.

It was really humbling to hear my pastor say these things about me. As Mike was ending this introduction, the blood in my head started to thump as it had many times before. I was instantly pulled away. As Mike was talking, his voice faded out, and a child's voice took over. "You're it," one boy screamed as he pushed the other. They both took off and ran through what looked like a large back yard in the country. One boy stopped at the well and was looking down it. He yelled to the other to come over. They both looked down the well and yelled into it to hear their voices echo. The older boy stood up on the edge laughing as his younger brother urged him to get down. The younger boy reached to grab the older brother, and as he did, he tripped and pushed his brother and then watched in horror as he fell into the dark abyss.

Next, I could see the same small child running into a kitchen to his mother, screaming at the top of his lungs. The mom was washing dishes as the boy approached her and screamed the words, " Nick fell into the well, Mama! He is in the well!" Dishes crashed to the floor as the mom ran as fast as she could out the door and across a large field. She fell just as she was getting to the old well and scampered

John 14:15

to get up and reach the edge of it. She screamed the name Nicholas down into the darkness as loud as she could.

The deadness of nothing came back. The silence was broken only by the little brother's crying. The woman yelled the name again and again but never heard a reply. She finally ran inside and called the police and then ran back to the well, yelling over and over again until the rescue team arrived.

My vision jumped to a man bringing the limp body of a little boy up from the well with the mom hysterically sobbing. I could see the other boy just sitting there in a daze as they worked to bring this smaller child back to life. Then I saw this boy standing as he closed his eyes and started to pray: "God, please, please, bring my brother back, please, please." He kept saying over and over again, "Please don't let him die."

At that moment I realized the eyes of that little boy were the same eyes I saw in Dr. Russell. That boy's prayer was answered. His brother began to vomit up the water and breathe in air. The mom almost passed out with joy, and her other son couldn't stop looking up and smiling, knowing his prayer had been heard.

The vision then jumped to a later time as Dr. Russell was reading his Bible and studying in school. He was in college and then speaking at large events, and then back to reality I came as quickly as I had left.

Mike immediately said, "You see what I mean? That's what happens sometimes. He drifts off as if he is watching something we can't see."

As I came back, I could only turn to Dr. Russell and tell him, "It wasn't your fault, you know." Dr. Russell was taken aback, and Mike was lost. But I said it again: "It wasn't your fault, that day at the well."

The man's eyes began to widen as he realized I knew something I couldn't have known. "What are you talking about, son? Is this is a joke?" he said.

"It's not a joke, sir, and it wasn't your fault that day with your brother."

As the shock continued, tears rolled down his face, he could only say, "Yes, it was."

"No, it wasn't," I insisted. "And God answered your prayer regardless, right?"

He began to smile between the tears, and the words "Yes, He did" came from his mouth. It was as if that whole incident had been the reason for his life's work.

Dr. Russell turned to Mike and said, "I have seen enough, Mike." He then swung around back to me. "I want to offer you an opportunity, son. I want you to attend the university and get your degree in ministry, specifically in apologetics. I believe this day was divinely planned, and I want to obey God's will. You can do the work online, but I want to stay in close contact with you through this journey if that's okay with you."

I wasn't sure what to say, and Mike was still clueless as to what we were talking about, but he was happy the meeting had gone so well. Dr. Russell spoke up again: "You don't have to answer me now, but go home, speak to your wife and family, pray intently, and call me as soon as you can."

As we walked out, I knew before I left the church grounds that God had shown me what He wanted me to do, not only with my life but also with the gift He had given me.

This realization gave me a lot to think about. I knew this gift was something that was in me before I was saved. I had done nothing to earn it. But now, after surrendering to Christ, I finally realized what the gift was to be used for. This again reminded me of how blind I was before my salvation, not just to my gift but also to all of life around me. I had gone from living for myself to living for God and others. I wanted to tell people about how awesome it was to be free from myself and from that blindness. I had a growing excitement about this new life that had to come out one way or another, and I was glad it was there. I had finally come to the point that I had a purpose and that I was part of something much greater than myself.

Over the next three years, our life changed tremendously. I took the courses for the degree in ministry, and we had to start having the small group meeting at the church since it was growing in numbers every week.

What I most remember are the questions people asked — both saved and unsaved people. Question after question they asked. There were so many, and as we worked through each question, I wrote down the answers we received from the Bible and our discussions and kept a record of them. I got them organized in such a way that it almost looked like a book, and the funny thing is, that's exactly what my wife thought. She said, "We should do it. Let's get it published!"

I was finishing up college, and I was excited about graduating. I'm not really sure why since I didn't know yet what I was going to do with the degree.

My pastor had hired me on as a part-time anything and everything guy. I was learning so much from him, and the church was exploding. It all happened so quickly, and as people kept coming, a little more each week, we were making plans to renovate the church building.

In regard to the book, we decided not to even put our name on it. It was just *Truth,* written by A. Nobody. We thought this was a clever way of not letting the reader associate the truth with an author but rather with God. Ava worked night and day on the revisions and even put little stories at the end of each chapter so the reader could associate the question with a real-life experience. When she was finished, we sent it to a publisher almost as a whim, not thinking we would ever hear from anyone and really not caring much whether we did.

Chapter 11

Psalm 139

The day started out great. It turned into one of those days that burn into your memory and you never forget. Scooter was turning six that weekend and Spencer four later that year.

Ava was at Wal-Mart buying groceries, and Scooter was in the seat of the cart, still just little enough to ride there. If she tried to let him walk, he always seemed to find his way under the cart, where he tried to lie on his stomach as she pushed the cart through the store. As she was turning a corner, Ava turned her head away, looking for some milk from the dairy aisle. Suddenly, a loud clang rang out as another cart slammed into the front of hers.

The woman pushing the other cart was a middle-aged lady with nice hair and even nicer clothes. Ava didn't know whether to smile or be alarmed. The woman gave no apology or reason for hitting the cart, and she was showing no emotions. Later, as she told me what happened, Ava described the next few minutes as a blur.

Ava quickly realized the woman whose cart had hit hers was Mici's mom, Wanda. She was standing in front of Ava, and she started talking with no introduction or excuse for her rudeness. She must have recognized Ava and hit her cart on purpose. She obviously had something on her chest, and she was determined to get it off as she shot the words across the cart. Ava never budged.

Wanda's tirade began in a surly way, and it was clear to Ava as she listened that this woman looked down on her, as if Ava were some piece of white trash. She was filled with hate for Ava and began to tell her she was garbage and that what she had done to her son was unforgivable.

"You may try that innocent act on someone else, Ava, but it won't work on me," she said. Then she looked at Scooter in the cart and said, "I see you didn't have much trouble moving on."

At those words, Ava immediately transformed into something she had never known before. Seven years of something had been bottled up in Ava, though she really hadn't known it was even there. But now it began to come up, and it came forth in epic proportion. Ava came around the cart and grabbed Wanda by the shirt collar and pushed her against the bread rack. The words that came next from her sweet lips made Wanda realize she was not talking to the person she expected.

The words came out as if from a loudspeaker: "Your son raped me! Do you hear me? He raped me! I didn't ask for it, and I didn't want him to do it, but he drugged and raped me. What he took from me that day was not his to take, but because of your money, he got

Psalm 139

away with it. So understand this: if you are looking for sympathy from me for your son's sins and your own, I have none to give. But if you're looking for a fight, I will give you all you want."

Wanda could not speak, and as Ava let her go, she stepped back in shock. Scooter was not sure what to think, but he never cried. He just stared with big eyes. He had never seen that side of his mom before. When Ava looked at Scooter as she was leaving, she almost burst out laughing at his wide eyes and his mouth gaping open at what he had just seen. What I realize now is that was Ava's day of reckoning. God allowed that confrontation and provided the inner strength to face her enemy, and she needed that.

Wanda began to tear up a little, and it seemed as she looked back at Ava, she realized that what Ava had said was true and she knew it deep down; she just didn't want to deal with it.

It seemed almost as if someone whispered something to Wanda before she left, and it caused her to turn and look back one more time, not at Ava but at Scooter. As she glared at the young boy, the fact that Scooter was her grandson seemed to click in her mind. Scooter looked like his dad, and Wanda knew it.

Wanda turned and left without saying anything else, but Ava knew it was not over. She knew Wanda now knew that Mici was the father of Scooter and that this was only the beginning.

One week later Ava and I received two letters in the mail, one was from an attorney representing Mici's family, and the other was from the publisher concerning the book.

Life has a funny way of serving us its delights mixed with a little bitter and a little sweet. I guess the only question is which you taste first.

We didn't know which one to open first, but we finally decided to look at the publisher's letter first and get a little sweet taste to offset the bitter. The letter was short but to the point and gave the cell phone number for the representative to call as soon as we could. The letter stated the following:

Dear Mr. and Mrs. Keith,

It is my pleasure to send you the enclosed contract. As stated in the contract, we would like to send you a check in the amount of thirty thousand dollars for the first installment of your book, *The Truth*. We are so very excited to make you this offer and would like to meet with you as soon as possible to express our plans for sharing your wonderful message with the world if you decide to accept.

Ava and I sat there speechless, taking in this wonderful news we really did not expect. We were so happy and shocked, but we could not fully enjoy it, knowing the other letter was there waiting.

We opened the second letter, and Ava began to tear up as I read it. It basically said that Mici and his family wanted to know if Scooter was part of their family, and if so, they wanted rights to him.

The idea of having to deal with Mici ever again was a mountain in front of Ava, and I felt helpless. I looked softly at Ava and said, "We will use every penny of that money to get the best lawyer we can to make sure this does not happen."

That evening we called the pastor over and showed him both letters. He was as shocked as we were, but he seemed to focus on the letter from Mici's family more.

"About this letter, guys, I just refuse to believe that this is happening for the wrong reason. I know this seems like an enormous mountain, but I want you both to quit looking at how big the mountain is and start looking at the beauty of it instead."

"Beauty?" I snapped back. "What beauty is there in this?" I was taken aback. My emotions were high, and I was in defense mode, thinking of Ava.

"Funny you should ask that, Collin, since you're the one with the gift to see through people and realize the truths in their situations. Collin, I want you and Ava to see through this mountain and find out what God wants you to find in it. What is He accomplishing through this passage on this particular mountain? By the way, has He not already provided a lot of tools to accomplish a victory? He is not leaving you empty-handed on this trip. He has equipped you for a purpose and given you this mountain is for a purpose, so let's find out what that purpose is."

Mike had a way of putting things that made you feel secure in Christ no matter what you were facing. Ava was immediately at peace, but I was just a little less stressed. My fear of sharing Scooter was greater than my faith in God at that moment. I didn't want to see beauty in this mountain; I just wanted this mountain to go away. I wanted to destroy this mountain and walk over it as it lay beneath my feet.

I knew from before that Mici had issues from his dad's pornography as he was growing up. At that time I felt a little compassion for him, but it was mostly anger now. I didn't care about any of them. I also would never allow that legacy of sexual imprisonment to be put on my son, regardless of who his biological father was. I was his dad, and I was going to protect him from that at all costs.

As I was in thought, Mike had begun to read Scripture to Ava. He was reading about Peter stepping out of the boat and walking on the water toward Jesus. When Peter turned and saw the waves, he started to sink. At that very moment, I could feel myself sinking in this disaster. Then Mike read the most wonderful thing: Jesus reached forth and held Peter up and said, "Thou of little faith." He then brought Peter back to the boat.

Jesus didn't let His friend sink. I knew now my issue was not that I didn't believe in Jesus but that I believed in the waves or the mountain more. We prayed, and I felt assurance that we would overcome this and would be better for it.

Mike had called most of the church to pray for us, and I could feel the Lord holding us up and encouraging us to have more faith. The confidence and assurance kept coming the following day in church with the message about Paul and Silas going to prison for casting a demon out of a lady.

The man who owned this particular woman was irate at the two followers of Christ for doing this, so much so that he had them beaten and taken to the centermost part of the prison. This guy sure must have had some pull in his time. I associated the story with Wanda and Mici's family trying to get custody of Scooter.

The reason for the man's anger in the Bible was that now the demon was removed, the woman could not produce income for him through her fortune telling. The story goes on to say that in spite of all that had happened to them because of doing the Lord's work, Paul and Silas began to sing praises in the night air of that prison. They worshiped God in their storm. That is when I realized we must do the same. When Paul and Silas worshiped instead of worried, the earth shook, and the jail doors opened, and the shackles fell off.

I remember thinking that if that had happened to me, I would have been gone. I would have high-fived myself and done a little shimmy shake as I danced out of that place, but Paul and Silas didn't. They didn't leave. They just sat there. But why not?

The prison guard knew he would be put to death if the prisoners escaped, and assuming they had escaped, he was about to kill himself. That's when Paul spoke up and told him, "Don't worry; we are all here and are not going anywhere." The guard then realized he needed the God these two men had, and he asked Paul what he must do to know that God.

Paul took that moment of tribulation and turned it into an opportunity for salvation; he then led the man to Christ. The man was so overwhelmed with appreciation, he took Paul and Silas back to his house and washed their wounds and fed them. That evening the man's whole family was saved, all because Paul did not leave the storm until he realized why he was in it.

I vowed that same thing after hearing the message. I would not try to get out of this storm until I knew why God had me in it.

After weeks of visits to a very sharp and articulate lawyer the church found for us (at no charge by the way), he made us realize that at the end of the day after all the smoke had cleared and all the arguments were over, if Mici had enough time and enough money, he would be able to be a part of this child's life.

I know this devastated my wife, but she seemed to have a peace through it that I did not have. It even scared me a little, thinking maybe she had some kind of plot in store and that if the judge allowed Mici visitation, she might pull out a gun and shoot Mici and Wanda in the head. It honestly made me a little happy thinking of that possibility, as far-fetched as it was however. I had to pull those thoughts away, knowing they were doing no good.

Finally, I asked Ava the night before the court hearing how she could be so calm. Her response was genuine, as she looked at me with those big green eyes. She said, "I know my child Michael will never leave me. Mici took something from me that night that was not his to take. It was not his to take, and I didn't want him to take it.

He took that from me out of his own selfishness, but God used that horrible deed to give me Michael."

Michael was asleep in her lap, and she stroked his head as she was telling me this. She went on to say, "If God can take what Mici did out of sin, addiction, or whatever else and then turn it into this (looking at Scooter), then there is nothing He cannot do. I love this child, and I know God loves me even more than I love him. I will trust in His hands, and I will walk this road, but I know He will not abandon us."

I just sat there in amazement at her, and my doubts and my questions seemed to fade away instantly. But what did not fade away was the hate I still had for Mici.

We got up the next morning, but before we left for court, we received a phone call from the publisher. He explained that we needed to talk soon. "The book is ready for final print, but I need you to review it as soon as possible," he said.

We told him we didn't know what was to come of the case, so he said he would send it in the mail overnight so we could get it as soon as possible. He ended by saying, "I realize the timing is not good, but I need it back within two weeks, regardless."

As excited as we were, the book wasn't our focus. We were preparing for the biggest day of our lives up to that point. Scooter and Spencer were still asleep, and Ava's mom and dad had come up to help and support us through this. Ava's dad was going with us to court, and I was glad. He was a godly man, and I liked the fact that he was on our side. We had grown pretty close over the years, especially after I got saved, and they were actually thinking of moving back to be closer to us and the grandkids.

As we entered the courtroom Mici, his mom and dad, and his lawyers were already there and all together at the table in a huddle. As soon as Mici looked up, he focused solely on Ava. She didn't flinch but looked back at him square in the eyes, as if to say, "You're outmatched."

Mici was not the same arrogant stud he once was, however. It was clear that the lifestyle he had been living had caught up with him. He couldn't even look Ava in the eyes for more than a second.

We had heard he was expelled from college for failing grades and drug possession and had to move back home. Looking back now, I am sure this was all about his mom's agenda and not his. He could barely take care of himself. He could hardly care for a child. It almost seemed as if he didn't want to see that his past had found him yet again.

The mom and dad, however, were a different story. Mici's dad was stone-faced, and his mom was almost giddy as the proceedings started. The judge began with the formalities of this type of case, and the lawyers chimed in. The legal terms seemed to go over most of our heads.

What did get our attention was when their lawyer said they were looking for joint custody of the child. I wanted to scream out, but I looked at Ava and she never blinked. Our lawyer began his part and said we did not want any visitations accepted and that before the judged ruled at the end of the case, he wanted both parents checked by a therapist and given a drug screening.

When he said this, we could see the distress on the faces of Mici's parents, and the lawyer immediately said, "Your honor, we would also like to state that regardless of the findings on the father in this case, the grandparents have rights as well to see the child."

Mici's head just sank, realizing he was in way too deep. It was obvious he was exhausted. At that minute, as if someone were helping him up, Mici shot straight up and said, "Your honor, can I talk to you with just my lawyer, Ava, Collin, and their lawyer?"

Immediately Mici's mom stood up and shouted, "You wait a minute, Mici! What are you trying to do here? Mici's dad looked at him and grabbed his hand to pull him down, but Mici pulled back and screamed, "No! No more!"

The judge quickly put a stop to the drama. He spoke first to Mici's mom. "Ma'am, I would advise you to sit down and be quiet. If I hear another word from your side, this case is going to be over very quickly. Do you understand?

"First, I am granting the request that both parties will comply with evaluation and drug screenings. Second, I absolutely would like to meet with each of you privately and see what we can do to get some resolution here."

Just then, Wanda started to speak again, and the judge quickly pointed a finger at her and said, "I would not advise that." She reversed course immediately, and we all proceeded back to the judge's chambers.

The office was not very large, and I did not like Ava being so close to Mici. He already looked defeated, however, and I again had to fight feeling more sympathy for him than anger. I hated that I felt any sympathy for him, for it made me feel weak.

The judge looked at Mici and said, "Son, what do you want to say?"

Mici immediately began to tear up, and the first thing he did was look at Ava. "I am so sorry for what I did, Ava. If I could take it back, I would, but I can't. I don't want to hurt you are anyone else again."

The judge interrupted. "Son, are you admitting to something here?"

"Yes sir, I am," he replied. "Your honor, seven years ago I took Ava on a date, and I laced her drink. After she was incapable of resisting, I raped her." Fighting to say the words, he said again, "I am sorry for what I did, but I can't take it back."

Mici then turned again to Ava and continued, "I am sorry. It was like I was being controlled by something else, and I am tired of fighting it. I give up. I don't want to cause you any more pain. Judge, I don't deserve and I'm not fit to be any part of this child's life. My mom won't stop, though. Your honor, I need help. I need help for myself."

As he finished talking, I could not believe what I had just heard. It was like a weight had been lifted from the entire room.

Before Ava could respond, the judge looked at her and said, "Ava, you have some choices to make. First of all, I am willing to grant no visitations of any kind to anyone in that family. Second, I want you to know that upon Mici's testimony today, he has admitted to an assault on you, and he can be tried for that assault. Double jeopardy will only apply to other charges. I know this is a lot to answer so quickly, but what do you want to do? If you need some time, I will grant it. We can reconvene latter today for your decision."

Without batting an eye, Ava slowly turned and looked at Mici and took his hand. My eyes widened, and he immediately began to weep uncontrollably. She softly said to him, "First, Mici I want you to know I do forgive you."

Mici could not handle this, and neither could I. All of our eyes were filled with tears. Mici just kept shaking his head, saying, "No you don't. You can't."

Ava continued, "Mici, I do forgive you, and I want you to know that there is someone who can help you. His name is Jesus, and He is greater than your problems."

"I have done too much. I don't deserve it," he sobbed.

"We have all done too much," Ava replied, "and none of us deserve it, but you said you wanted help, right? You let Him into your heart Mici, and He will bring you help. If you really want help, then you have to let Him in to get it."

All Mici could do was slowly nod his head yes. His hand dropped from Ava's, as he held his hands to his face in disbelief. The judge said, "I would like to make a suggestion if it's okay."

The judge was glassy-eyed as well but fighting through it to maintain control. He said, "Son, there is a detox and rehab place I know of that can help you if you're willing to go. I will make sure they accept you, and based upon your release and how things go, Ava can then decide about pressing charges."

Mici quickly nodded his head yes. Then Ava continued, "Your honor, I would also like to say if he does go through this, I would like to permit visitation to him and his family, based completely on my authority, if that's allowed."

The judge looked at Ava and said, "Ma'am, after what you did in here today, I will give you whatever you want." Neither lawyer said a word as the matter was finalized.

When the judge went back and told the court what his ruling was, Mici's parents were not too happy, but I believe for the first time Mici's mom realized she needed to support her son and not continue to bully him.

Before we left, Ava tapped Wanda on the shoulder and with a soft voice said, "If you would like to meet with me soon, we can talk about visitation." Wanda almost lost her breath right then and there but quickly said yes and left the room.

As we left the courtroom, Pastor Mike said he wanted to show us something. We followed him back to the church. When we walked into the gym, we couldn't believe what we saw. There were at least a hundred and fifty people, all on their knees praying for us, for Mici, for the entire situation. We both lost our knees a little and almost fell to the ground.

When Mike proclaimed we had won, the roar in the room was deafening, and we could feel the excitement from every corner. We spent that evening celebrating the victory. We had seen God take the worst day of our lives and make it one of the best.

The next day came quickly, and we were still reeling from the day before. We decided we just wanted to spend time at the house with the two boys all day long. We played games, ate lunch and dinner together, laughed, and just relaxed as a family. Later that night Ava and I finished reviewing the book and sent it back to the publisher the very next day. We really didn't care what happened next. We were just loving life and looking forward to the future together.

Chapter 12
Solomon 16:11

"Wake up, sleepyhead. It's time to get up again. We got a lot to do today, so get up!" I screamed. I rubbed her back as she slowly stretched and completely dismissed my scream, knowing it was not real. As I kissed her on the neck, I said, "I know just the way to start this day." Ava giggled because she knew what I was up to.

Just as Ava rolled over to say, "I bet you do, pervert," I felt a little hand smack me on the face, and I heard the sound of another one a little older, laughing at me for getting smacked.

It was Saturday, and the sun was bright. I grabbed them both and roared like a lion, as they screamed to get away. We lay there and laughed for a minute, and then I looked at Ava. "Hey, what's for breakfast?" I asked.

The reply was, "Whatever you make," as she tapped my nose with her index finger.

"That's not being very submissive, you know."

"Well, I was submissive enough the other night for at least a weeks' worth, don't you think?"

I could never get one over on her; she was always a step and word ahead of me. God sure gave me a woman with a quick tongue and just for laughs a unique ability to see completely through me.

I came back with, "Well, it seemed you enjoyed yourself as well the other night."

"I did," she said, as if I had asked a question. "It's all part of my servant hood to you, sweetheart—sometimes good and sometimes not so good."

I immediately ended this discussion since it was not moving in my direction and it was obvious she was up for the challenge more than I was.

I got up and ate some cereal with the boys, and we showered and dressed. We did have a lot to do. The list was long. We had to get things packed for a much-needed vacation. It was the first time in five years, and how we ever did need it. Myrtle Beach was the destination, and it was only a three-hour drive, which made it even better. We had a house rented. It had a pool and was right on the beach. Ava's family also was coming for a day or two, and I was looking forward to the low country boil (sausage and shrimp, corn, potatoes, seasonings all thrown out onto a table just ready to dive into).

Before we could leave, though, we had a graduation lunch. I had finally graduated with my masters in apologetics. I had been working very closely with Dr. Russell, especially the last few months.

Dr. Russell was trying to talk me into moving to L.A. and starting a renovation church. I didn't know what that was until he explained it in more detail. It is a church that renovates lives. It has services and programs, but its sole purpose is to make disciples out of individuals. I thought that was what church was supposed to do in the first place, but this was different.

The preaching, the music, and the programs were all designed to work with individuals to make them disciples, not just church-goers. So many other churches were just places to hear great music and great preaching, but the quality time leaders spent with the followers was nonexistent. These show churches were springing up everywhere. The pastor would be preaching from one place, and his video feed would go to another church, where they would see him on the screen. Large crowds, awesome music, and great messages, but not many disciples were coming from this. Happy Christians, yes, but everything seemed to be focused on the leader's ability to entertain, not on the power of Christ.

Two things Dr. Russell said about the new church movement has stuck with me over the years. The first was if the message cannot be preached anywhere, then the message needs to be changed. The feel-good preachers don't like to preach about the blood of Jesus, the cross, or anything negative for that matter. Although I find some of these guys very motivating, this for-profit style preaching has no substance in the trials of your life. I realized if you eat only the icing, you never get to the cake, and eventually all icing makes you sick.

Second, these satellite guys were trying to take over the masses through their technology and entertainment value. If the pastor died or went away, the whole ministry would surely dissolve in a short matter of time.

Based on this Dr. Russell was encouraged about the idea of a renovation church. As much as I loved the concept, my current church was already like this, and I just could not see myself moving to L.A., so I politely refused the offer. It frustrated him, because he knew we were onto something with this idea.

As the graduation lunch ended, we loaded the car, and off we went for what I was hoping to be the best vacation ever.

At the beach it was just as I wanted: peaceful and warm. I sat on the beach the first evening with Scooter and Spencer and watched them play in the sand. Ava was cooking the boil, and it smelled perfect. I remember just thanking God for everything and realizing how much we needed Him in our family.

Ava's mom and dad had arrived, and as we came in for dinner, Poppy, or Granddad, quickly said, "Lets go looking for some crabs, kids."

They were all for it, and Ava yelled, "Don't stay too long; it's almost time to eat, guys."

As they left, I sat back on the couch and laughed at Ava and her mom talking about getting into bathing suits the next day. Ava started doing the moves she had been learning on the Brazilian butt exercise DVD she had been using. They both looked back at me and laughed when they realized I had been listening. Ava's mom came and sat down and just smiled as if to say, "Life is great."

I asked how things were going, and she replied, "Great," and we began to talk about everything that had been going on. As she was talking, I felt my mind pulling me away.

The vision started in a medical building, and sitting in an office was Ava's mom and dad talking with a doctor. I heard the doctor say, "Brenda, I am so sorry to tell you this, but the cancer is aggressive and is in stage four. There is not much we can do. There are options, but I am not sure any of them would delay the outcome. I will give you some time here, and I will come back in a few minutes."

Ava's dad was still in shock and could do nothing but say no and shake his head. Brenda laid her head on her husband's shoulder and said, "Baby, we knew this could be one of the answers. I don't like it, but we live for Him, not the other way around."

They cried, and I could feel my eyes filling up with tears as I came back to the present. Brenda looked at me strangely. She realized I knew. "Please don't tell Ava yet. I need some time," she said. I wiped my eyes as Ava walked into the room. We quickly changed the subject as the kids came in and we all sat down to eat.

Solomon 16:11

The meal was fabulous, just as I had anticipated, but the idea of Ava's mom being so sick made it hard to enjoy it as much as I had hoped. As I prayed that night when Ava was fast asleep, I felt the need to go outside and just sit on the beach and talk to God.

I found a place in the sand to sit. The moon was full and shining off the water. No lights were on anywhere, and in a way I felt like I was alone in the world.

The conversation that took place was not expected, but that's usually the way it went when God and I talked. I would tell Him all my thoughts and plans, and then He would show me a better one.

I remember saying, "God, I don't want to complain, and it's really hard to while looking at all You have given me and all You have created, but why do You have to take Brenda? She means so much to us, and she does so much for You here. I just don't understand You sometimes. I love You so much, but what could it hurt to let her live? Anyway, more than anything, just please stay close to both of them and give us all the strength to get through it. You know how much Ava loves her." As I was just about to get up, Spencer touched me on the shoulder, and I almost jumped out of my skin he scared me so badly.

I caught my breath as he sat down and laughed at me. Some protector I am, I thought, as he continued to laugh. I had been talking so intimately with God I thought it was Him, I guess.

As he sat down, I stopped thinking about anything and was just content with the beauty of the moment with my son. I hoped I would never forget that. Just then Spencer looked up at me and said, "Dad, what's heaven like?"

At first, I was taken aback by his question, but then I realized the answer, as if someone had written it on my heart for that very moment. "This is what it's like, son. It's being with your dad and your dad being with you," I said.

"What about the streets of gold and all that stuff?" he quickly responded.

"It's true. It says that in the Bible, but the real value of heaven is not so much that as it is about being with the ones you love and the ones who love you. The rest is just God's creation on display, just like tonight." God had just given me the answer I had been looking for. Who was I to ask God to prevent Brenda from being a part of that sooner rather than later?

I realized I was being selfish in my request for her life and decided I wanted to hear God more than I did myself. We went to bed that night, but that memory will forever be etched in my heart.

The rest of the week was much the same. The night before we left, Ava started feeling nauseous. She went to bed early, and I woke early to the sound of her throwing up in the bathroom. I went to check on her and realized I was not much help, so I left her to herself and the porcelain god she was wrapped around.

As we were getting ready to pack up, we sat down for a quick bite of breakfast. As usual, the boys were messing with each other;

flipping Froot Loops at one another was quickly becoming an Olympic sport at our house.

Ava came in and went to the kitchen. She slowly placed a few eggs on her plate and came and sat down. I noticed she had something in her hand, but I didn't want to mess with her too much in the state she was in. As I ate my bacon and kept to myself, she leaned over and whispered something in my ear. As I heard the words coming from her soft voice, I accidently sucked a piece of bacon into my wind pipe and began to choke. I finally got it up, as they were all laughing at me hysterically.

I did not feel my death was that funny, but it was quickly forgotten as she said, "You did it again, dadeo," and placed a little white stick in my hand that had a big blue plus sign on it.

The blood continued to rush to my head, and I quickly replied, "What? How did this happen?"

"What happened?" my boys replied.

"Mommy is pregnant again, boys." I was stupefied at the moment and said it again as if I were completely ignorant to this knowledge, "How did this happen?"

My boys quickly chimed in and started saying the same thing: "Mommy, how did you get pregnant?"

Scooter just said, "Great. You better go get some more breakfast. I bet the baby is hungry too." He then added, "It better be a girl; I am tired of boys."

I slowly sat back down, realizing how and what I had just heard. Ava's mom and dad were laughing and smiling at me. They had already learned moments before I did. I slowly turned to Ava and then looked at Scooter. "You're right; we do need more food." Spencer just kept asking how it happened but finally gave up when no one answered. We drove back from the beach that day, and Ava was glowing as we drove home. When we got back, we unpacked and I just relaxed.

I guess I didn't even know how much the pregnancy would change our lives. I don't think anybody does for that matter.

Ava's mom came over later that week and told Ava the news about her cancer. Much to my surprise, and as much as she cried at first, Ava just seemed to enjoy her mom even more after that.

The days passed quickly, and Ava's mom passed away in just three short months. We struggled to answer the boy's questions, but Poppy stayed with us and we stuck together, and that was good enough.

We needed some good news, and we got it when we found out the book was selling really well. Things really took off, however, when a talk-show host got hold of a copy. What happened next went beyond anything we ever imagined.

It all began when we were headed to the ultrasound appointment. I was excited, hoping to get a girl. These boys were great, but just like Scooter, deep in my heart I really wanted a girl as well. They finally called us back to the room, and we waited patiently for the doctor.

We could see the talk-show host talking on the TV, but the volume was down, so we couldn't hear anything. My phone was ringing every second, it seemed. I really thought it was broken, but I finally answered it to see what was going on. It was our publisher, and he said, "Collin, look on channel 4. I hope you're sitting down, buddy. Your book just hit the big time: TV."

"What are you talking about?" I said. I hung up and slowly turned the volume up on the TV.

We both watched in amazement and were speechless as the talk-show host went on to say, "Who are you, Mr. or Ms. A. Nobody? We want to talk to you." She held up the book again and said, "We will find you and see if you're for real."

As the commercial came on, the doctor came in. He saw we were in shock and quickly asked, "Are you guys okay?"

"Yes, we're fine," I said. We didn't bother mentioning what had happened.

"Well, I have something very important news to tell you, and you might want to sit down, Collin." This brought us both back to reality quickly, for he had a very serious look on his face. He slowly looked up and said, "There is something going on with Ava and the baby. We have confirmed what it is, but there is nothing we can do about it."

Ava looked at him as he hesitated to say what it was. "Well, what is it?"

With a big smile from ear to ear, he said, "Well, it looks like your baby has a roommate, and they are both boys."

"What? How did that happen?" I said.

Ava barked over at me, "Collin, I think you know, okay? Enough with the 'How did that happen?'"

I just shut up for the moment. It was too much to take in anyway, and it felt like God had made my life his personal gag reel. Finally, I just smiled and kissed Ava on the head. "Is this for real, Baby."

Chapter 13

1 Corinthians 13:1-7

We had fifty messages on the answering machine when we finally got back home. As we listened to each one, it seemed almost like we were in a dream. We didn't create this book thinking we would ever receive this response; we didn't need or even want the attention. The good news was the money from the book royalties would be going to missions, which gave us a feeling of making a difference, and we liked that. The attention, however, was considerable and we were just a regular family. We were out of our environment.

The last two messages were the ones that really got our attention. The first was from Dr. Russell, congratulating us and then expressing an idea he had of how to make the church discipleship idea work in both places. He suggested we talk soon, but basically he was saying that I would preach the sermon, and he would run the video feed from my service to his and have them both taken care of simultaneously.

This was not a new idea, but what was new was the program outside of the service, the discipleship maker's component. This was the difference maker for me. He wanted to meet early the next week, and he would come to us this time.

The last message was from the producer of the talk show we had seen. He asked if I could meet in Chicago soon to discuss an interview and what we should expect. He left his number and asked that we call ASAP. We called the next morning and got a voicemail, so I just left a message telling him to call back when possible.

We had just finished eating breakfast when my phone rang. I reached for it to say hello as Scooter and Spencer argued over who had more cereal in his bowl. "Hello," I spoke with one hand over my other ear so I could hear better.

The voice replied, "Collin, this is Mark with PPG network affiliates. I think you know this already, but Kelly is thinking about having you on as a guest on the *Kelly Live* show." Kelly had the number-one rated talk show on daytime TV and had her hands in a lot of things socially and globally. I was pretty stunned at this request, even though I knew it was coming. The only thing I could think of as he was talking to me with the boys yelling at each other was, "Why us?"

"Why what?" he asked.

I didn't realize it, but I had spoken what I was thinking without knowing it. I hate it when I do that. Finally, I said, "Please hold on, sir." I turned to Scooter and Spencer and said, "If you two nut jobs don't both hush up and quit fighting, the next cereal you see will be tomorrow morning. You got it?" They quit fighting, but then I heard Mark on the other end of the phone saying, "Hello. Hello. Are you still there?"

"Yes, Mark, I am here. It's just a little chaotic around here I guess."

"You asked me why, and to tell you the truth, I am not sure how to answer that," he said. He then immediately continued: "Kelly does not spend too much time discussing religion issues, but she is really interested in the truth issues. Just so you know, Collin, she does not agree completely with your book but she wanted me to let you know that regardless of her opinion she would be fair to you if you would consider meeting to discuss a show. There is also the thirty thousand dollars you will receive for this if that makes a difference."

I asked Mark if he could give me a day to think about this since we were not the Hollywood type. But I promised him we would consider the request seriously. I told him I wanted to talk with my wife.

He quickly said, "You're married, are you? That's interesting."

"Why?" I asked.

"Well, to be truthful—no pun intended—we were placing bets on who A. Nobody was. So far I am not doing so hot.

"By the way, before you go, Collin, I read most of your book, and I have to tell you, I am not sure about God and religion and all that stuff, but I was inspired by the stories. You definitely have caused me to take a deeper look at what I believe to be true. Just so you know, I think it's made me a better person, so thanks for whatever that's worth."

"You're welcome, Mark, and I will talk to you soon."

I hung up. My wife, who was also trying to get the kids straightened up, heard only part of the conversation and was excited to hear the rest.

"Well, what did he say?"

"What did who say?"

"The guy on the phone."

"What guy?"

Ava quickly drew back her hand with a wet rag in it, and I am sure it was coming my way unless I gave in and finally told her.

"They want me to speak on the *Kelly Live* show."

"What? Are kidding me, Collin? That's the biggest talk show on TV. What are you going to do?"

"I don't know. I was going to ask you and Pastor Mike the same thing."

Mike and his wife came over that evening, and we had a wonderful dinner and even better conversation—about the request for the talk show but more so about the babies coming. With everything going on, I had almost forgot Ava was pregnant again. When we ended that night and before they left, Mike asked if I would say a prayer, so I did. It was prayer of thankfulness, not about a successful book or even a pregnancy but more about closeness with God and a feeling of following His will. It was a prayer of thankfulness that He cared enough about us to give us a life. I will always remember that night; it is burned into my brain. In that very moment of prayer, I thought of Fredrick and the family he left behind. I promised myself I would call them the next day, just to say hello and to remind them of what he meant to me.

The next few weeks flew by, and we accepted the invitation to the show. I had a 9:00 a.m. flight that Monday to meet Kelly face to face for lunch in Chicago.

I got to the Westin Chicago River North hotel right off Dearborn Drive around 11:00. Chicago was a beautiful city, at least from where I stood. The hotel was right against the river, which runs straight through the city. I went out on the walkway and just stared at the water and all the buildings that made this town such a tourist magnet. There were shops and places to eat everywhere, but I had to get ready since I was meeting Kelly at 1:00 at a place called Shaw's Crab House. The driver was picking me up in an hour, and I was pretty nervous to say the least, not about the book or what I was going to say, but more about the newness of everything. As I walked back toward the hotel, I realized why they call Chicago the Windy City. It was November, and I had on only a thin coat. When a gust of wind hit me, I could feel my face burn from the stinging of the cold. I gained a new definition of cold that day, as I hurried into my room to get ready.

The driver met me downstairs and put me into a large black sedan, the kind used for driving executives and important people around, I assumed. The driver didn't say anything, so finally I asked him how he was doing.

"Good sir. How are you?" he replied with a half-smile.

"Getting accustomed to things, I guess," I replied.

"Well, you'll fit in just fine, I'm sure, sir. Here in Chicago we take all kinds." He had a way about him that was smooth and calming.

As we reached the restaurant, I asked him his name and handed him a tip. "Rodrick, sir, but I can't accept your tip. They have already paid me, but thanks anyway." As I was leaving the car, he said, "I will be here for you when your lunch is over."

I entered the restaurant, and the smell was mesmerizing. The waiters wore jeans but tuxedo tops. It was a very appealing place.

The hostess asked how she could help me, and I said, "I am here to see Kelly."

She quickly realized who I was and said, "You must be Collin."

"Yes, I replied.

"Please follow me, then, and welcome to Shaw's."

We circled the place, and I was finally led to a small room in the back with doors that closed from both sides. As I walked in, a very sharply dressed man stood up and said, "Hello, Collin. I'm Mark. It's good to see you."

Kelly was there as well, but she never got up. She reached her hand out with an intentional smile. "Welcome to our city, Collin. I hope everything has been accommodating thus far."

"It has, Kelly, and I would like to say thank you, before I forget, for the hospitality you have shown me."

"I wouldn't thank me just yet, Collin. This conversation may not be what you expected."

"Well, that's fine with me, because I wasn't sure what to expect anyway."

She smiled, and I quickly realized she was just like everyone else, just a person playing her role in this life. We sat and went through some formalities as they took our order.

I didn't want to eat a lot for lunch, so I ordered the crab cake and thanked the waitress for her time. When the food was delivered, I noticed the waitress seemed quite nervous. "What is your name? I asked her.

"Tami, sir." She seemed scared by the question, so I kept going: "Tami, just so you know, you are doing a great job. Before we eat, I am going to pray. Is there anything I can pray about for you?"

My question seemed to bounce around her mind, and she paused before answering, She finally seemed to relax and said, "Yes, please pray for my little boy. He is really sick, and we need some strength."

She was tearing up, so I said, "Okay. What is his name?"

"His name is Toby, and he is four."

"Okay, Tami, you stay with us as we pray. Is that okay with you, Kelly?"

"Absolutely," she replied quickly, but it was not as if she really had much choice.

I prayed, "Father, I lift Tami and Toby up to You at this very moment. They need You, Father, and we need You as well. God, I ask You to give Tami Your strength, and I pray, God, You would heal her little boy, Toby. It is obvious, God, Tami and Toby need You. Your Word says that if we ask in Your name, we will receive it, so that's what we are doing; we ask this request in Your name, Jesus Christ."

As I ended, Tami was smiling but tearing a little too, so I told her I was sorry and I didn't mean to mess up her day. I just thought she needed prayer. She hugged me and whispered, "Thanks."

As Tami left, Kelly looked at me. "Collin, are you for real? Is this who you really are? I have seen a lot of people try to be things they weren't, and I have to tell you I believe at least you are sincere if anything. I am just trying to see if there are any ulterior motives.

I waited for a moment and then said, "Kelly, I am a mess of a man. I guess I have made more mistakes in my life than anyone. The only thing I seem to be good at is loving people, so that's enough for me, I guess." Mark just smiled as he took in our conversation.

The food was beyond delicious, and I wanted to ask for more and would have if it were just my family. In the middle of eating, Kelly laid her fork down on her plate, looked at me and asked a question that obviously had been plaguing her for some time now.

Do you think because you prayed that prayer, Collin, that her child will really be healed? Your book says things like this as well, but to me it seems like fantasyland. Kids die every day, and they have been prayed for. What makes one different from another?"

1 Corinthians 13:1-7

As the words were coming out of her mouth, I could feel my mind pulling me away. I tried to stop but, as usual, to no avail. It was a rush of pictures at first—pictures of Kelly as a little girl, her mom swinging her at a park, then picking her up and hugging her when she came home from school. I saw her mom giving her a doll at Christmas and putting her on her lap. I saw them walking and spending time in the park. But next I saw her mom lying in bed sick with Kelly lying on top of her, crying. Her dad picked her up and took her out of the room as Kelly kicked and screamed. Her mom was saying, "Baby, it's okay. I love you. It's going to be okay." Then I saw Kelly, still a little girl, on her knees praying, begging God to save her mom. Then she was at the funeral, looking lifeless and numb. As the vision was beginning to fade, I saw her go into her bedroom and knock the Bible off her nightstand before lying down to sleep.

As I came back, Kelly was looking at me and finally said, "Collin, are you okay?"

"Yes, I am fine, Kelly."

"You didn't answer my question," she said. "Will that child be healed because you said that prayer?"

I thought for just a second and realized why she was asking this. Finally, I said, "Yes, Kelly, the child will be healed but not just because of my prayer. The question is not, *Will* the child be healed? It is, *Where* will the child be healed? Will it be here on earth, or will it be in heaven?"

This answer caused her to sit back in her chair. "Hold on. That's not the same. How can the death of the child be the healing?"

"Our definition of healing and God's definition are very different sometimes," I said. "The truth says that God's healing is not a temporary healing just so someone can spend a few more years on this earth. God's healing is a healing of permanency, a healing that will never go away, and that is true healing. Kelly, the world wants everything done the way we see fit. We all die, and it's the ones left behind, like you and me, who have to deal with the loss. If God chose to heal that child by bringing him home to Him, is that unfair or unacceptable? Actually, that is the greater healing, is it not? Our problem is that our focus is on this life, and that is not the focus of the Bible or Jesus' message.

"Let's put it this way, as a primitive example: this life is like a movie trailer. I love movie trailers. I actually get just as excited about seeing them as the movie itself, so it doesn't bother me that there are so many before the feature. But they are only trailers, not the movie I came for. The trailer is part of the experience, but the reason I came to the movie was for the actual feature showing. Our life is like the trailer, preparing us for the real movie coming up next."

She laughed a little and then said, "Okay, I see your point, but it seems to me that regardless of what happens God is never to blame."

I didn't reply as I knew the answer and hoped she realized what she had said.

1 Corinthians 13:1-7

As we left the restaurant that night, I couldn't help but be burdened for the young waitress and her situation. I prayed again that night for her and her little child, but I realized I also had to believe what I told Kelly was true. I went to sleep knowing what is truth is not always easy to deal with and it is not always what is best in *my* opinion. At the end of the day, though, I would rather God be all truthful and things go His way than mine. I have seen what my ways do to a life.

The next morning the driver, Rodrick, rushed me to the show. Again, he didn't say much but was calm and had a smooth smile on his face, almost as if he owned the city. I asked him before I got out of the car, "Rodrick, are you a Christian? Just curious."

He turned back at me with that same grin and dark eyes and said, "If I'm not, will you still like me?"

"Yes, of course," I replied. "Do you still like me after asking you that?"

"Absolutely," he responded.

I never got my answer, so I just closed the door and walked into the building. As I was walking in, I thought it strange that I didn't get my question answered, but I felt like did in a way. I almost wished I could have discerned Rodrick, but there was no time for that. I had to get to the taping.

I entered the building, and a young intern helped get me settled. She told me the taping would begin in about forty-five minutes, and I was to wait in the room. Individuals kept coming in and out as I waited. The makeup person came in, and I said, "Please, not much if any."

She laughed and said, "Sir, you need a little for sure. You'll thank me later, I promise." She was a pleasant girl but a little too forward for my taste. Why did she call me "sir," I wondered. Was I now becoming a *sir*? Now that I think about it, though, who was I to question her about this? She was the expert on who needed makeup and how much or how little.

Next, the director came in with Kelly to go over the game plan. Kelly sat down on the large leather sofa in the room. "Okay, Collin, this is how the show will go. I will interview you and ask questions specifically about the new book. You should keep the answers short, but I won't cut you off either. We have only so much time, and I want the audience to be able to ask questions as well. Are there any questions you have? Are you nervous?"

"I'm a little nervous, I guess," I replied, "but actually I am intrigued by all this and a little excited too."

"What do you mean?" Kelly questioned.

"Well, I just find it fascinating how God seems to allow things to happen in such a way as to get us to places in our lives, crazy places we never dreamed of being, especially for A. Nobody like me." I laughed, but they didn't, so I reminded them of the author of the book. I finally just shut up.

As the show began, I waited backstage. After the introductions, Kelly finally announced, "Okay, Mr. A. Nobody, come on out, and let's find out who you really are." There was no turning back now. I walked slowly out to the small, polite applause of the crowd. I wondered, Why are they really clapping? Have they even read the book, or are they just going along with everyone else? Is it just because they are on the Kelly show? I had to admit, though, I would rather they clap than sit in silence. I sat in a middle-sized, comfortable chair, and Kelly welcomed me. Then the conversation began.

"So your real name is Collin, correct?"

"Yes."

"You are married, and the pastor of a church."

"Yes, I'm married, but I'm not a pastor. I'm more of a teacher at our church. The pastor, however, is awesome. Hello to Mike by the way."

Kelly laughed and said, "Is there anyone else you want to say hello to before we start grilling you on this book, Collin?"

"Well, sure, if you're going to let me. Hi to my beautiful girlfriend-wife Ava and my boys and everybody back in South Carolina. I'll be home soon, and I miss you bunches."

"Your girlfriend-wife, huh? That's interesting."

"Yeah, I try to think of her as a little bit of both; it keeps me on my toes." (Back home I was sure Ava had her hands over her face telling me to shut up.)

Kelly continued, "We might come back to that one, but let's get to the topic at hand. This book you wrote, Collin, *Truth*. Isn't it a little presumptuous to say you have the answers to some of humanity's biggest questions, questions that generations have debated with no real resolutions? Yet you claim to have the answers right her in a few pages."

"Well, I see what you mean, but really my book is just answers to my own questions. I didn't provide the answers; God did. I just wrote them down. These same answers have been there all along. I just found them."

"So God spoke to you, and told you to write this book? Does he speak to you often?"

"Absolutely. Lately, it seems like He speaks to me in everything. I don't hear a voice like I hear yours, but I get His message just as clearly as I get yours."

"How is that?"

"Well, let me put it this way. You have friends and people in your life you are close to, and when you grow to know a person well, such as a child or husband or wife, you learn to hear them without them ever saying a word."

"But that is an adapted language you assume based on past experiences, right?"

"Yes, and that is part of what I am saying. I have spent a few years listening to God, and I am still learning more about Him every day. He doesn't come and go. He is always right in my ear, so very close. It's a great feeling actually. I do ignore Him sometimes, but His Spirit is always present and lets me know He's there. And I don't believe I am unique in this either, Kelly. Anyone who is a follower of Christ has this same Messenger with them as well. I guess some people just ignore Him better than others."

"You are pretty bold in your book when it comes to some heavy topics, Collin. For example, you assert there is only one way to heaven and that it is a sin to be gay, and you purport to explain why there is suffering in the world. But how do you know that what you have written is absolute truth? In fact, how can you say that real truth even exists at all? Everyone has different circumstances, upbringings, and cultures, and we all are very different. It seems to me that truth is where each person finds it." The crowd began to clap as she ended. I am sure it was a coincidence that we went to a commercial then.

At the break, Kelly turned to me and said, "You're doing great, Collin. After your response, I will let a couple of the audience members have a crack at you; then I'll have one more question.

As we were waiting to go back to recording, I said a quick prayer: "Father, I feel Your strength, but I need Your words. I need Your wisdom and Your truth, not my own. Please know I love You and thank You for this life. I want to be your vessel."

"We're back," Kelly announced. She then repeated the end of her last question.

At that moment I could feel the Spirit quicken in me as my reply seemed to come from deep within, from a place I didn't know was there.

"We are all so different, Kelly, just like a family with many different children—all different but with one father and one mother.

You see, the truth is in the father, not the kids. The father teaches the children the rules of the house. He sacrifices for each one so they feel loved, secure, and fed. And, most important, each one knows he is the father and he is responsible for them. The rules don't always make sense to the children, but they do to the father and mother. The problem is that we associate imperfection with everything, and it is hard for us to believe there is such a thing as one perfect Father. Each child has a unique relationship with the father that differs from that of his or her siblings, but the father never changes. He is the trunk, and it is the children that become the branches."

Kelly thought for a second and finally replied, "So I see this explains that the same truth exists because the Father stays the same. But doesn't that mean all roads lead back to this one Father. So every religion has its rules, and that's okay because everybody is tied to the trunk of the same tree, right?"

"Therein lies the problem, Kelly. You must accept Jesus' death on the cross as payment for your sins. When you do that, you become part of the tree. Before that, you're not His child; you're not even part of the tree."

I heard some grumbles from the audience, and Kelly quickly said, "Okay, this is a good segue to our audience. Let's get some questions from them."

She turned to a young man who was standing and holding a microphone that had been given him. "What is your name, sir?"

"Christopher."

1 Corinthians 13:1-7

"And what is your question?"

"I am a gay man (the clapping began in the audience before he could even finish his sentence), and I read your book and did enjoy some of it. But how can you say it is a sin for me to love another man when I was born that way? I have always felt attraction for other men, and I don't think a loving God would call my loving someone else a sin in anyway." The crowd again clapped and then waited for my reply.

"Christopher, you do seem like a nice guy, and there is no question God loves you tremendously; but He has a greater plan for us than we have for ourselves. I have desires in my life—even strong desires—that I don't fulfill because God tells me not to. God's Word tells me how to live my life, and it is my job to follow Him to see if what He says is true or not. But what is not my job is to change what He says to fit my desires. When we decide to do things that contradict His ways, it is like saying, 'Dad, you're wrong about this one, so I am going to do it my way, but you will be okay with it, right"? Christopher, your life is not just about your needs being met and your happiness; it's about how you affect the entire community, nation, and world you live in. Even nature itself shows us that life is created by a man and a woman, male and female, x and y. God designed the world this way, and you have taken it upon yourself to change His ways to fit your ways."

"Next question," Kelly said.

"My name is Vickie."

"And what's your question?"

Vickie trembled as she spoke and seemed very upset as she began. "I was a Christian, and I loved God, and I agree with almost everything in your book, but God lied to me. Seven years ago my little boy was four years old when he was kidnapped by a lunatic. He was raped and killed before they found him." The woman began to sob uncontrollably as she finished. "My family is still devastated to this day. I can't remember how much I prayed to God for help and how many Christian friends told me God would deliver him. When he was found, those same friends had the nerve to tell me it was part of His greater plan and I would see him in heaven one day." She began to get angry and much louder as she said, "I don't want to see him in heaven. I want him now!"

The audience was silent, and for the first time I actually felt this was the opportunity to reach some of them. Before, it was all just a show, but now it became real and we all wanted an answer. I got up and walked to the woman's seat. I kneeled down so that I was lower than the woman, and I looked her straight in the eyes. I felt her pain, and I could feel the tears welling up in my own eyes. "Vickie, you said you were once a Christian, and I believe that. Would you give me the opportunity to pray one last time before you completely give up on God? I think this is where the answer lies."

She nodded her head almost exhaustedly, and I grabbed her hand and began to pray. "Father, Your child is in need of You. She needs to know her little boy is safe." I could hear her begin to sob. "God, please let her know that he is with You and she is with You too. Father, show her she is not alone and You will never leave her side. God, we live in a wicked world and nothing happens without Your allowing it. We want to know why You would allow this to happen."

I stopped to listen for just a second, and I felt the Spirit gently comfort us as the response came: "He is mine now, Vickie, and I have never left your side. I didn't want that man to do that, but I allowed it, just as I will allow you to die one day. He is happy with me, and you will be too. I will never leave you or forsake you."

As soon as the Spirit spoke to us, Vickie wrapped her arms around my neck and squeezed me way harder than I imagined any woman could. She told me she had heard His answer. "He is happy" was all she could say.

The audience roared, and half were in tears. They refused to stop clapping, and finally Kelly just went to a break. I sat back on the stage, and Kelly came back beside me. "Try not to leave the stage again, okay Collin?"

I quickly replied, "You tell God that. I was just following directions."

We came back on the air and Kelly began, "I have one last question, Collin, and before I ask it, I want to thank you for sharing with us today. My question is this: If what you say is true and the book has the answers you say it does, do you believe you are some sort of prophet or messenger of God?"

Pride rushed into my soul, and I realized this was the moment Satan was attacking me. I knew if I answered with any note of assurance that I was some type of prophet, I would be received in a great way by many. My mind began to envision the fame and fortune that would lie ahead. I wanted to say yes, but a gentle voice reminded me of who I was. I slowly looked up at Kelly and said, "There is only one messenger, Kelly, and it's not me. He is Jesus, and He loves you, and He loved your mom and every one of us more than we can imagine. I am A. Nobody, Kelly, and I am fine with that. But He is not. He is a somebody that we all need, and He is here for all of us today."

Kelly ended the show and asked if I would stay and sign autographs for my book. She gave everyone in the audience a copy, and it seemed most stayed to get it signed. Many asked me that day what they must do to know God, and I was thrilled I got to share with each of them His truths. As I got into the car, Rodrick had a big smile on his face all the way back to the hotel; and as I got out, he said, "It's great when the Spirit does the talking for ya, isn't it?"

"Yes it is," I said. We then shook hands and parted ways. I left that evening to fly home and could not wait to get home and see my family.

Chapter 14
John 16:33

The last few months had been a whirlwind. We were trying to get the room ready for two babies, and the phone was ringing off the hook about the book. I realized it was a book that spoke to the masses, but I never imagined this.

All the calls were not pleasant, though. One Monday I got a call from a young man named Megale—at least that's who he said he was. At first he seemed pleasant enough, but then I realized he was not a raving fan. His words were, "Who are you to say that Jesus is the only way? You can't prove that, and you deserve to die for saying it." Then he hung up. I didn't tell Ava. I knew it would only upset her. After several other threatening calls from followers of other religions, I finally got our phone number changed to an unlisted number and stopped answering my cell phone if I didn't know the number. The good news was that when I got such messages in my voice mail, I would block the number, and that seemed to help.

I woke Ava up the next morning early; we had an appointment with the doctor concerning the babies. Ava was getting quite big, and the babies were only two months from being born. On our way to the appointment, Ava kept asking what names I liked. I finally said, "Baby, I have a hard enough time remembering the two we got. She turned her head, and I heard her began to mumble a little. I felt like a jerk. "I'm sorry, baby," I said, and I rubbed her shoulder.

She quickly turned with a big smile and said, "I know you are, but it's okay. I still love you." She got me again, and she just laughed.

When we got to the office, they led us back to the examining room and had Ava lie on the table. The doctor came in and said, "Okay, guys, let's take a look at these little monkeys." As he moved the ultrasound probe across her belly, he seemed to look a little concerned, so much so that I asked if everything was okay.

"To be honest, guys, I am having trouble finding the heartbeat of one of the babies. Please don't be alarmed yet. I want to admit you, Ava, and run some test before we draw any conclusions, okay?"

Dr. Miles was a great doctor, and his concern was genuine. I called Ava's dad immediately and asked if he could watch the kids. He said yes and said he would bring them up later.

Ava was admitted, and they started doing a battery of tests. Her dad came shortly with the boys. The boys and I were in the room when they brought Ava in from one of the tests. She smiled when she saw the boys. Spencer asked, "Mom, is everything okay?"

John 16:33

"I hope so," she said. She smiled and grabbed his face and gave him a kiss.

Scooter was almost ten now, and he realized something was going on. "Mom, I promise I will be praying for you," he said.

I then said, "How about we do that right now, buddy. Would you do the honor?" He smiled and nodded his little brown-topped head up and down.

As we held hands in that small room, Scooter began to pray one of the most affectionate prayers I have ever heard. He started by saying, "God, I know You can do anything You want, and I am asking You to please keep my mom and brothers safe so they can come home with us. God, I know You love us, and if you do this, I will do whatever you ask from now on." This was the first time I saw Ava cry about what was happening, but it was more of a proud-of-her-son tear than a scared one.

As he finished, Ava's dad opened the door, and the doctor followed right behind. He asked if he could speak to us alone. Poppy took the kids to the house, and I promised to call them later.

Dr. Miles sat on the foot of the bed and spoke. "There is no easy way to say this, guys, but one of the babies has no heartbeat. I am so sorry, Ava. If there was anything I could do, I would, but there just isn't. The other baby is fine, and this will not cause a problem for him, but I do not want to take the other baby before your full term, just to be safe." When Ava asked how much longer, he said three weeks. I could tell Ava was exhausted, and the doctor left us, telling us to feel free to call him for anything.

As we sat there in the semi-dark room, I was very confused about how to feel. Knowing one child was alive and Ava was okay gave me peace, but I felt remorse for the other child I never got to meet.

"What can I do for you, Ava?" I asked.

She looked at me with a confused look. "I am full of grief, but I really just want to praise God, Collin. Is that horrible? I feel guilty for wanting to. What's wrong with me?"

"Nothing, Ava. If we can't praise God now, then what kind of love is it we have for Him?"

I was just as confused. The one thing that pressed my mind was what I was going to tell Scooter. I had taught him that God hears our prayers and answers them, but this was not the answer we wanted. I stayed with Ava that night, and the next day the doctor let her go home. He said he wanted to see her once a week for the next three weeks to make sure all was going okay with the other baby.

The next morning I walked outside to see what the day was going to be like, and the sun was already blistering and the humidity was creeping up with every tick of the clock. The idea of one of my children passing away was weighing heavier and heavier, and I could no longer push it out of my mind. I went back into the house, where Ava was cooking breakfast. It smelled great, and I was excited to see she was feeling well enough to do this. I went into the kitchen and wrapped my arms around her waist and leaned in to smell her neck and kiss her softly on the cheek.

She drew her head back as if she were in some movie, saying, "Yes, my love, I am yours." She had not lost her sense of humor.

I asked, "Are you okay?"

"You mean besides the fact I am about to explode? Yes, besides that, I am good; but I do want to say something. I want to make sure we have a service for our baby, okay?"

"Absolutely," I responded, and as bad as it may sound that was it as far as discussing the situation from then on. We went back to the doctor each week, and each time he said all was okay. We scheduled the delivery for the week following her last visit.

I got home the next night, and as I lay down, I saw the message light on the answering machine blinking three messages. I almost didn't push the button, but I did anyway just to get it over with. The first message was from Dr. Russell. He offered his condolences on the baby but reminded me of the blessing of the one that would live. He said they had the plan laid out for the new church and wanted me to give the first sermon. He seemed very excited and reminded me it was going to be broadcast all over the country.

The second message was from the publisher, telling us we had been nominated for a writer's award and to call him as soon as possible.

The last call was a strange voice on the machine, but I had heard it before. Soon I realized it was the same threatening voice I had heard before, now telling me I had no right to force the Bible on anyone and that my day was soon coming to an end. I saved the recording and decided I would get the police involved the next day. I sat down with Ava and told her about the threat, and I went to the police station around 11:00 a.m. the next day to report the incident.

I walked in and found a very attractive young lady sitting at the front desk. She looked up and asked if she could help me. I told her who I was, and almost immediately she began to smile. "I will get a detective to help you, sir." She returned and said, "Someone will be with you in a moment." I few minutes went by, and she said, "Mr. Keith, I just want to let you know your book made my life better—well, not just your book but Jesus, I should say." I felt relieved when she added those last words, as it always made me uncomfortable when getting a compliment on my book.

She spent the next few minutes telling me the change that occurred after she and her husband accepted Christ. Just as she was finishing up, a deep voice from the back came out from behind a white wall, "Please send him on back, Sherry."

She quickly thanked me and then quietly said, "Pray for him. He needs Jesus, a lot of Jesus." I snickered as I entered the room but quickly realized the man did not seem too happy to see me.

"Hello, Collin. I am Detective Tony Maker. How can I help you?

I explained what had been going on with the threats, and he recorded our conversation. When I was finishing up, he turned the recorder off and said, "Collin, I want to be honest with you."

I quickly replied, "That's always a good way to start a conversation, I guess."

He wasn't amused, so I decided to just listen. He continued, saying, "There is really not a lot we can do about threats, especially if we are not sure who it is. You need to continue to listen to the messages and get as much info as possible until we can identify this guy." I told him I understood and that I would keep him informed moving forward.

He then said something that caught me off guard. "Just so you know, if you keep writing that stuff, you're probably going to get a lot more of this kind of thing."

"Stuff?" I replied. "You mean the book?"

"Yes, the book. I mean preaching is one thing, but when you start telling people there is a real God and a real truth and Jesus is the only way, don't you think you're just encouraging this attitude in a way?"

"Detective Maker, all I wrote was the truth. I realize it's not the most popular thing, but it is important, I believe."

"Collin, there is no truth, only opinions. You can tell people whatever you want, but I live it on the streets, and I find it really hard to believe in a God who allows the kinds of things I have seen." As he continued, I felt myself being pulled away. I really didn't want this to happen as I was trying to engage with him, but it happened just the same as always.

I immediately saw Tony sprinting after a man. He was sweating profusely, as if it had been chasing him for a while. He followed the man into a small alley and up some steep stairs. The man ran into a dark building, and Tony followed.

Tony stopped. He could hear footsteps, but there was no light. As he moved down the hall slowly, trying to be cautious with every step, he could hear the man yelling almost hysterically, saying, "Hide the children! Hide them all! They are coming! They are coming!"

Tony pulled out his flashlight and opened the door that led to the yells. As his flashlight pierced the room, he saw the man was standing there, hovering over a small body, telling the children to run. Tony realized the man was not in his right mind, so with his gun already out and aimed at him, he yelled, "Freeze now!" The man looked at him and then headed straight at Tony with a knife raised. Tony yelled again, but the man just kept coming. The man had no intention of stopping, and Tony quickly pulled the trigger twice.

The man's body fell lifelessly, and Tony quickly checked to see if he had a pulse and was still alive. He realized the man was dead, and he immediately looked for a light switch and flipped it up.

As the light glowed in the room, he surveyed the area and realized where he was. The man had brought him back to his abandoned apartment. It was a rundown building and, as he soon discovered to his horror, a place where many children had lost their lives. As his backup arrived, I could see the anger on his face. As Tony searched through the apartment, he saw a Bible lying on the coffee table. In a fit of anger, he picked it up and threw it across the room.

As I came back, Tony was asking me if there was anything else I needed. After taking all this in, it took me a second to reply. "No, sir," I said, "but I want to say something before I go." I stopped. I just couldn't think of what to say or how to say it. Finally, I just said, "Never mind." I left the office in despair but hoping and praying for another chance to speak to Tony one day.

I got home, and Ava surprised me with a candlelit dinner. She had taken the kids to her dad's place for the weekend, giving us some alone time we really needed. We talked that night about everything, including what I saw earlier with Tony. I told her how seeing that made me appreciate the health and safety of her and the kids more than ever. After listening to the horrible things I saw in that apartment, Ava reminded me of that particular case. She remembered seeing it on the news a few years back. There were over twelve children found that night, all dead and dismembered.

We went to bed early, but I woke up in a cold sweat. I could still see those bodies lying there in the room. I closed my eyes as I lay back. "God, would you please help me to understand how you could allow something like that to happen."

The answer was not coming nearly as quickly as I wanted, and I really wanted some clarity.

In my mind I said, "If you're going to protect anyone, God, shouldn't it be them, the innocent ones?" I couldn't sleep, so I finally just opened my Bible and read. John 3:17 caught my attention: "For

God did sent not his Son into the world to condemn the world; but that the world through him might be saved."

I breathed deeply as I read it and realized we were the creators of evil, not God. Man is to blame for these horrific happenings, not God. Just as I put the Bible down and was thinking on the scripture, I heard a creak in the living room. Ava was asleep. The blood raced to my head, as I realized somebody was in our house. I listened and could hear the footsteps coming slowly down the hall. I grabbed my baseball bat, not sure what was coming next. I thought I should stay in the room, but I wasn't sure, as I wanted to separate myself from Ava.

I opened the bedroom door and stepped out into the hallway to see where the noise was coming from. As I looked down the hallway, I heard the shot ring out. I felt the bullet hit my shoulder, and it knocked me backwards into the wall behind me. The adrenaline ran through my body, and instinctively I lunged at the figure coming toward me. It was like I was someone else; my anger was kindled above any fear I could feel. I was angry and didn't care what happened to me; I was determined this person would not hurt Ava. As I dove at him, we both fell to the floor. I heard Ava scream, "What's going on?"

I was on top of him, hitting him with one punch after another. I felt his nose break with one of the blows, as I came down on top of it with my fist. I grabbed him by the throat and was trying to kill him, to take his life. I wanted him dead, and I felt his life leaving him as a voice in my head said, "That's enough." Ava was now watching, and again I heard the voice.

Ava put her hand on me and said, "Collin, it's okay! We're okay. Don't do it." I didn't want to stop, but the anger subsided when I saw him go unconscious and I finally let go of his neck.

I quickly turned him over and rushed to get the duct tape from the kitchen. I taped his hands and feet as many times as I could and then called the police. I had forgotten I was even shot until Ava yelled at me and said I was bleeding. The police and paramedics arrived, and I had to go to the emergency room for treatment.

The adrenaline must have deadened the pain. The bullet had gone completely through my shoulder, and all that was needed was cleaning and stitches.

As I sat in the hospital ER, Tony walked in with a smile on his face, but shaking his head. "Glad to see you're alive, Collin. I'm sorry you had to go through this."

"Yeah, not nearly as sorry as I am. Who was that guy anyway?"

"We are getting all that done, but I can tell you this: it was sure lucky you only got shot in the shoulder."

"Well, I don't believe in luck, Tony."

"Yeah, I know," he quickly replied with sarcasm. "Jesus saved you, right?"

"Let's just say He empowered me to fight back."

Tony paused and then finally said, "I will give you this for sure: most people are in shock when they get shot, and they freeze up. I'm glad you didn't. One less crazy on the street, you know." As Tony started to leave, he stopped short and looked back. "You still believe in a God after seeing somebody like that?"

I sat there for a second and finally replied, "I believe God saved me tonight, Tony, and I believe He loves that man as much as He loves me. The only difference is that I have Christ and he doesn't.

"Tony, don't give up on God or judge Him for people's bad decisions. There are a lot of evil people in the world, but God came to free us from this. He came to help us become what we can't be by ourselves." Tony just continued to shake his head as he walked out the exit.

Chapter 15

Job 1:21

August 27, 2001, Cooper Reed finally entered this world. He was our third son, and we could not have been more blessed. As the doctor handed him over to Ava, his eyes never left hers. He stared at her without the slightest blink. He was so beautiful.

His brother was delivered just a few minutes later and was pronounced dead immediately. We named him Anthony Scott, and he was put to rest the following weekend when Ava was strong enough to move around.

As the weeks passed after the birth, we were busier than ever incorporating another addition to the family into our lifestyle. Reed fit right in, and the other boys didn't seem to skip a beat.

Intrigue over the book just seemed to grow and grow, so much more than we ever expected. More checks came in. We were cautious to not let the money control us; however, it was tempting to go buy things we didn't need. As a family, though, we really just enjoyed the simple things, like eating dinner together, ball games, picnics, laughing at one another's little quirks, and just normal, inexpensive family activities. The book continued to sell well, and we were asked to speak at larger and larger crowds, not only about the book but also about our story as a family and what we had been through.

As the book's impact grew exponentially, my ability for discernment seemed to grow stronger as well. As I spoke to people more and more, the visions increased. They did not occur constantly but much more often than in the past. What I came to realize was the more I allowed myself to care for others, the more this happened. I still couldn't control it, though; it always came when it wanted and without my regard.

I continued to get death threats, especially as the speaking engagements grew larger. As the crowds grew, I finally had to include a detail to watch over my family and me before, during, and immediately following these messages. I was constantly being asked to speak on talk shows. There were so many requests we had to limit ourselves to one per quarter. As unbelievable as all this was to me, what was most amazing were the salvations that were taking place.

God always showed up, and I believe people just felt the freedom of the gospel. Ava, thank goodness, kept me grounded through all of this. She always reminded me how God uses the most incapable to do His work so that He is the one glorified. When I asked her what she was trying to say, it was always the same answer: "God is just so great when He uses you, honey. It's like he is just showing off."

Job 1:21

Time continued to race by, and the boys were growing rapidly. Ava and I really enjoyed this time in our life and were actually working on another volume of the *Truth* book. As life so awkwardly does, drama came pouring back into our lives, but this time it was not just my family but an entire nation that was rocked to its core.

It was August 3, and I was asked if I would give a message in New York the following month. I accepted, and my wife and I were excited to get to see the city together. We planned to do everything—Chinatown, Little Italy, the Trade Center, and the Empire State Building. The date was set for September 22. Little did we or anyone else know then that a day eleven days earlier, Tuesday, September 11, 2001, would be a day that changed all of our lives forever.

The morning of that infamous day in history I watched the plane slam into one of the towers and heard the news of the Pentagon and the other planes going down. I saw the fire forcing people to jump to their death. It was the most horrific incident my mind could imagine.

I can remember the entire church gathering that evening to pray for the families of the lost and for the country as a whole. We were devastated at the loss of our fellow Americans, and there seemed to be nothing short of mass hysteria the following week. No doubt we had come to a turning point in the history of our country, and what we did next would decide our fate for the future.

The day following 9/11, I assumed the upcoming event would be cancelled, but as usual God had bigger plans.

On September 12, I received a call from the secretary of state and was told I would be getting a call from President George Bush the next day. He said I needed to accept the call—as if I wouldn't or even had a choice in the matter. I woke up that morning and got dressed. Ava and I sat in the kitchen. When the call came, I put it on speaker so we could both hear.

The president said hello and I froze. After a few seconds another hello came. Finally, Ava hit me, and I blurted out, "Hello, Mr. President." I felt like an idiot. Ava just grinned. "Hello, Mr. President. How are you doing, sir?"

"I am okay, son, but we have some work to do," he replied. I listened as he told me he expected a record crowd to be at the event I was scheduled to be speaking at. He said in no way should we consider cancelling it. "Our country needs God's message now more than ever, Collin, and it is obvious He wants you to give it."

As we hung up the phone, I was humbled and excited all at once, and then it happened. I realized I had no idea what I was going to say. I spent the next few days praying and fasting and pleading with God to give me the exact words to say as He had done so many times before, but to my fear He didn't.

Two days before we took a train to New York, I finally told Ava the fear and the silence I had been feeling. As usual, her words inspired the message I was to give.

Ava spoke to my heart that day as she said, "Collin, God has given you a gift to see the world and the hearts of humanity as He does. Don't you see that He wants you to tell His people who they are and who He is? He wants you to tell them life is precious and there are things worse than dying, like living as if you were already dead. He wants you to tell them that death is inevitable but that life is a gift."

Her words filled me with honor and power, and I started to think maybe she should be the one to deliver this message because I sure enjoyed it. What I did do after listening to her and God was to prepare a message as if it were the last thing I would ever say, and for all I knew it could be.

The morning of the event Ava stepped out of the shower and jumped as the security guys knocked and spoke from outside the door.

"I am never going to get used to that Collin," she blurted at me. I turned my gaze from the beach picture on the nightstand and just stared at her. I was blessed, not because I had a gift of discernment or financial security, or even a great family. I was blessed because I was ALIVE, not just breathing air but alive in Christ. I didn't care what happened for the rest of that day. I was just blissfully content in Him being alive in me.

As the time grew closer to the event that evening, I became more anxious. Ava let me know it was going to be great, but the weight of the circumstances was overwhelming.

The city was in lockdown and the stress levels were high. The president had ordered double security and patrol, but it didn't help my emotions. It actually made it worse. People just wanted normality back, and that was a problem, for it was not to be found.

What was to be found was an opportunity to give hope to a needy city and country, to assure them that there is someone who can help and that normality and peace could return.

As more bodies were found, the death toll kept rising, and so did church attendance. However, the damage had been done by the enemy. The blow was hard and direct and was meant to knock us out and almost did.

As a country we were now saddened by the loss of life, but instead of dividing us it caused us to come together. We were angry, and more than anything else we wanted revenge for this act.

With all this racing through my head, the still small voice of God kept whispering to me, "Make this message about Me and nothing else." At first I couldn't hear it, or I should say I ignored it, but it was persistent until I finally understood.

Thirty minutes before taking the podium, that same voice finally came through loud and clear. It was telling me that freedom, love, truth, security, and peace are all gifts that did not come freely but with a price. Our country paid a price to have these things. Battle upon battle and war upon war, lives were sacrificed so that we could have and enjoy these things for the individual and the entire country.

Christ was showing me that was the same price He paid. He sacrificed His life so that we could have not only all those things but also—and most important of all—victory over death. Death is what

Job 1:21

we were facing on this day, and it was victory over it that must be found. I remembered the scripture, "Death, where is thy sting?" It rang out in my heart.

One last kiss from my wife, and I was escorted up onto the podium to a sea of people. Silence filled the air, as if it were choking us all. I stood at the podium with cameras flashing. I looked out into the crowd at the dejected faces looking back at me. These faces were looking for answers, hope, something to heal the wounds.

I noticed there was know one really moving except one person in and out trying to get closer to the front.

All of a sudden I felt the rush of the spirit over whelm me, as I looked into the faces it grew stronger and stronger I felt the words coming up from a place I never knew existed. I felt the energy in the entire place begin to become electrifying and as the word reached my throat I let it go from my lips screaming it out, not just this crowd but as if I was yelling it to the entire world, the universe hearing it and the deadening silence was broke with a roar of the words WE WILL NEVER GIVE UP rang out as I lifted my hands to the release of it.

As the crowd roared and almost every hand was instantly raised the sound was deafening. As the sound continued to resound through the park I saw the man that had been moving to the front approach the security rope, I saw him pull something from his coat and next I heard a ring of a different sound pierce through the air.

It was followed by a sudden sharp pain to my arm and as if I was hit by a truck I flew backwards. It knocked me three feet unto my back and then I tumbled another few feet before I stopped.

Blood was rushing to my head and out of my arm. I had been shot, and panic suddenly flooded the crowd and the staff. Everyone was either running or scrambling to find protection. Two security guards jumped in front of me and lay on top of my body. Their weight was overwhelming. I wanted to get up but could not move until they released me.

The last thing I remember was thinking that this was my moment of death, but as fearful as it should have been, it was not. I thought it was actually serene.

It's strange how our greatest fears lose their strength when there is something stronger in control. I wonder if that is how Christ felt when from the cross He said, "Father, forgive them; for they know not what they do."

CHAPTER 16

Galatians 5:1

The following morning the *NewYork Times'* front page read as follows: "Freedom and It's Price." The article continued, more like an editorial than a news article.

Today we have seen freedom and its price. This is the same freedom our soldiers past and present have stood for with their very lives. The same freedom our forefathers showed us when they signed the Declaration of Independence. The same freedom that grew a nation of all races and creeds into what it is today, a melting pot of humanity.

This freedom does not come without a cost, without the highest sacrifice—a sacrifice by so many that has served so many more.

The terrorists of 9/11, as well as the shooter at last night's event in Central Park, could not take that freedom away with their small-minded actions. However, through their actions our freedom is honored that much more today. We are America, and we are the land of the free, the home of the brave.

The speaker at last night's event, Collin Keith, was shot by a not-yet-named gunman and remains in fair condition at NYU Langone Medical Center.

The article ended by recounting all the events that had taken place that evening and the arrest of a man in the incident.

I woke up hazy to the sound of my wife saying as she had before, "Wakey, wakey, time to get up."

I muttered, "Please don't smack me. I don't think I can take it."

She laughed almost with a cry as I responded to her voice.

"I won't, baby. I promise," she said. "How are feeling?"

I finally got my eyes open enough to see her beautiful smile and her even more beautiful eyes staring back into mine. "I feel like I've been shot."

She rubbed the top of my forehead and slowly leaned over and kissed me right beneath her hand. "I love you so much, Collin," she said just as a knock at the door sounded.

Two sharply dressed men came in and closed the door behind them. My wife stood up and looked back to see the two men in black suits enter the room. "Hello, ma'am," one of the gentlemen said as the other stood in silence. "I am Brandon Griggs from the FBI. How are you doing?"

"I'm fine. I am Ava, Collin's wife. Can I help you?"

"Ma'am, we are with the FBI and needed to speak with Mr. Keith if that's okay. You can stay if you like."

Reluctantly Ava agreed but quickly added, "He just woke up, so please not too much, okay?"

Brandon, obviously the lead agent of the two, spoke again. "How are you, Collin?"

"I'm okay—just sore, I guess."

"This is my partner, Dennis, and we are in charge of the investigation of the shooting that took place last night. We need to ask you some questions if you feel up to it."

"I'm okay, just waking up."

Ava interrupted after a glance at her watch, saying, "I would like to stay for this, but if you don't need me now, I need to meet my father, who is flying in with my children this morning. I'll be back later."

"The kids are coming, baby?" I spoke up.

"Yes, the kids heard their dad got shot on national television. They are pretty excited, and the fact that you're alive is just gravy. They want to see you."

I laughed and felt the pain run up my arm and into my head. "Don't make me laugh, woman. I can't handle it," I said.

Brandon quickly said, "Yes, ma'am, that will be fine. If we need anything from you, we will ask when you return."

"That's great," Ava replied as she leaned over me with one more kiss. Then just before she left, she said, "Suck it up, big boy. I need you healthy, so don't get used to all this lying in bed stuff."

As she left the room, I just thought how glad I was she was mine.

Brandon sat down in the chair while his partner stood there looking at both of us.

"They caught the shooter, Collin. His name is Henry Barnes. We have not released this information or anything in regard to his past or reasons for the attempted assassination as of yet. Collin, have you ever heard of this man or know of any reason he would want to kill you?"

I thought for a moment. "The name rings a bell, but I can't remember. I'm sorry."

"Well, to be open with you, this guy has no priors, no real family around, and won't talk to us yet. All we really know is this: he was a preacher or is a preacher. I guess he just doesn't currently have a church. He had several churches in the past but nothing now. We plan on doing some interviews over the next few days to find out more, so if anything comes back to you, let me know."

"I have to admit, guys, the last person I thought would try to assassinate me would be a preacher."

"Well, Collin, we run into some real nut jobs, so nothing surprises us much anymore. We are going back to interview him again, but right now all he keeps saying is he had no choice—whatever that means. By the way, I would not suggest this, but he did say he would talk to you and only you."

"Guys, I can tell you I am not interested in that right now, but if you don't get anywhere with him, let me know. Please just keep me informed."

"You got it. We'll do our job and get back with you. Hopefully we can wrap this up and get it over with soon. I am going to leave someone here for the next day or so until you leave."

"Thank you" was the last thing I said as they left the room and the nurse came in to change the bandages on my shoulder.

I fell asleep and woke up an hour later to the sound of Scooter and Spencer. They were talking to me in what they thought was a whisper.

"Hey, Daddy, we love you" are some great sounds after going through something like this.

"Hey, boys," I said, "I sure did miss you."

"We missed you too, Dad. When are you coming home?"

"Soon I hope. You taking care of Momma and Poppy?"

"Yeah, she's been pretty worried since she picked us up, but I told her getting shot in the arm was a whole lot better than getting shot in the head or stomach."

"I agree, buddy. Thanks for helping out."

Ava looked at me as if to say, "Stop encouraging them," but I couldn't. At this moment they were looking at me like a warrior or a soldier who had been wounded in battle. I actually loved it to be completely honest. They were seeing me in a different light, not just as a dad talking about God, but also as an action hero fighting for goodness.

"Hey, boys," Ava's father spoke up, "let's give your dad a little rest so he can get strong to fight some more bad guys, okay? Who wants pizza?"

I quickly realized I was overtaken by their stomachs. After some hugs and farewells, they left Ava and me alone again. The silence of the room was relaxing, only because she was with me.

It was late, and Ava had been gone for about an hour to get some sleep when I heard another knock at the door. I assumed it was the nurse, but it was Brandon coming back to get some more information.

"Hey, Collin, I know it's late, but this is the time that counts the most, so I need your help. This guy Henry Barnes is refusing to talk or even eat for that matter until he gets to talk to you. We told him no way, but I wanted to see if you were up to it in a couple of days before you left for home. He would be completely restrained, of course, but we want to make sure he was working alone on this for your safety as well as your family's. Everyone could still be in jeopardy if he wasn't.

"We spoke to staff members at two of his former churches and came back with the same story. He came to their church and was hired with great anticipation, but they said he changed quickly after being hired. I am not a big church guy, Collin, so I wanted to get your opinion on their feedback. This may take an hour, so I can come back, but I would rather get this done if you feel up to it."

"Sure, go ahead. Let's get this done," was my response. I wanted to get this behind me more than ever. Before we started, though, I asked, "Brandon, what did you mean by your not being a big church guy? Did you mean you don't like church or you just don't go?"

With a little smirk, he responded, "Collin, I can appreciate your interest in me, and it's almost comical that with everything going on you would even ask that, but can I get through this first?"

I quickly replied, "I will make a deal with you. I will give you as much time as you like tonight, but I want thirty minutes of your time when this thing is done with. Is it a deal?"

"Deal," he responded. Then he quickly jumped into his questions. "The first church was in a little town called Jonesville, South Carolina. You ever heard of it?"

"Yeah, I have, but nothing really comes to mind about it."

"Well, he preached there for about three years, and they really liked him at first. But then they realized he was not preaching things that went along with what they believed. Apparently, he really didn't like to visit his church members and was much more concerned about the sermon than he was about his congregation or the members of the church. They finally asked him to leave because the church was not adding any new members and were not getting the support they felt a pastor should give.

"This is when things started to spiral downhill, it seems. He got another job as a fill-in pastor for a church in Union, South Carolina, after this, and things really got crazy. He again started well, we were told, but then his preaching began to get erratic again.

"The head deacon said he started going off on tangents in the pulpit about politics, as well as heresy in the church. For months he would go on and on about preachers taking away from the true Word of God. He said they did this by saying that people have choices and freedoms when they don't.

"He began to say that God caused everything to happen regardless of the event and that it was our job to stop people from teaching otherwise. When this church got tired of his tirades and tangents, they also asked him to leave. We inspected his house and found a room filled with his plans on trying to assassinate you, Collin. He had articles and clippings from press releases not only on the success of your book but also of your news interviews.

"Well, Collin, this is all we have on him. We want a full confession, but he has not budged, so I will keep you up to date in the near future. By the way," Brandon said as he left, "Collin, if we don't get anything from him tonight would you be willing to come by the station before you take off back home?"

"Yes, if you really think it's necessary."

With that Brandon handed me his card and left with his partner, who continued to be curiously silent.

The next morning the doctors told me I would be released and needed only physical therapy for the next few months as my shoulder healed. As we left the hospital, reporters were all over the place. It seemed the *New York Times* article had taken on a life of its own.

I told the reporters to give me a few days and I would give all of them a statement and answer their questions. Brandon picked up my wife and me in an undercover sedan and explained the situation as we left.

"Collin, this guy has not cracked, but he finally said last night he would agree to give a full statement if he could talk to you. You don't have to, but if you would, this sure would speed up the process and we could put this whole thing behind us and move on."

I agreed, and we headed to the station, where they were holding him with no possibility of bail.

As we entered the station, someone showed Ava where she could get some coffee and a place where she could relax until this was all over. She kissed me on the cheek as she left with a usual, "Be careful, baby. I love you." She always knew just what to do and say, and her timing was perfect, or maybe I just realized how lucky I was to have her.

When we came to the room, Brandon went in first and I followed. There were two officers in the room, and they left with a wink from Brandon. As I entered the room, I saw sitting at the table a middle-aged man who looked obviously worn out and tired. The handcuffs were chained to a ring in the floor and gave him no room to move his hands above his lap. The room did not have much light, only two windows with bars, and the day was grey anyway, which made it that much dimmer.

As we approached the man, he looked straight at me with his eyes wide open and a crazed look, as if he didn't believe I was there.

Before he could say anything, Brandon raised his voice and said, "Henry, I am not here to play with you anymore, and you better not play with us. This is Collin Keith, the man you tried to kill three days ago, and you have ten minutes with him before you give us your statement. Do you understand?"

Henry just sat there and nodded his head at Brandon as we both sat across from him at the table.

At first I wanted to punch him in the face as hard as I could and shake him by his fat neck until he was lifeless, but I knew couldn't, nor should I. I was angry but more than that I was happy to still be alive and I had peace, knowing this man's desire to see me dead did not take away from God's desire to keep me alive.

The man slowly looked up to speak with a hate in his eyes I have seldom seen in my life. His nose turned up as his teeth gritted, and then he spoke. "This is your fault, you heretic. You should have died that night. I had you centered in my sites, and if it were up to me, I would shoot you again if I could."

After he said this and I did not reply or show any emotions, he seemed to relax some as he realized I was not going to give into him so easily. He began again, "I know who you are, and God will judge you for your lies. You tell people they have freedom to choose and

Galatians 5:1

that God allows them to have this freedom. It's a lie!" he screamed. "God chooses you and all things are done by Him exactly how He wants it done. Man has no freedom. We are already chosen to go to heaven or hell, and your place, I have no doubt, will be the latter of the two."

Brandon jumped in and said, "Your time's running out, Henry, so you better get to the point."

"My point is that this man should die for what he is preaching, and I gladly admit to shooting him. I just hate that I missed."

After these final words, I could see this man was completely consumed with this hate for me and the message I had been delivering.

I began to feel my anger growing stronger as my mind pulled me away quicker than ever before.

I saw Henry as a teenager. It looked like he was standing over a bed. A man I assumed was his father also was there, yelling at the sick woman in the bed. I was sure it was Henry's mom.

"It is your sin that has put you here, woman!" the man yelled out. "I cast this sin and sickness away." The man continued to yell, but Henry obviously was out of sorts, not knowing what to say or do. Finally, Henry collapsed on his mother's chest, but the man quickly threw him off of her onto the floor. "Get away from her boy! She is possessed!" he yelled. "Your adultery has caused this, woman. You must repent to enter the kingdom of heaven. You have disobeyed the Lord our God, and His wrath is on you now. You must repent!" His voice thundered until the woman finally stopped breathing.

When the man realized she was dead, he looked down at Henry and said, "This is what happens when you disobey God, boy. God did this, and He will do it to you unless you follow His ways and His ways alone."

Just then I came back as quickly as I had left. Brandon spoke up again and said, "Okay, that's it. Your time is up, and we are leaving. My partner here is going to go over your confession to this again, and you're going to sign it."

The man sat in silence as Brandon stood. I did not stand, however, for I felt the desire to tell the man something. I stared into his hated glare, and I began to speak to him. "Henry, you think freedom is a bad thing because you think it leaves you in control, us in control. I know God is in control of all things, but He gives us this freedom of choice so that our love for Him is as real as His love for us. Freedom is what He gave the angels, even though they decided to rebel. Freedom is what He gave Adam and Eve, even though they ate the fruit. Freedom is what Jesus had when He allowed us to crucify Him on a cross over thousand years ago.

"The Holy Spirit Himself is the freedom of God in us, running through our veins. This freedom can never be taken away, only shared or not shared. I choose to share it, and regardless of how many times someone like you tries to stop me, it will only drive me to share it more. Finally, Henry, freedom is what God gave your mother that night when she died, freedom from your father and his lies."

Henry's eyes got big, and I thought for a minute he was going to jump right over the table at me, chains and all.

I continued, "God did not cause your mother's sickness; this world did. Your mother's sins, no matter what they were, did not take away the freedom of salvation she had received."

His face began to break as I finished, but I never skipped a beat.

As I got up to leave, I looked at him and said, "Henry, what you meant for my destruction God used for my goodness. I owe God thanks, but to you I owe nothing except my prayers."

Chapter 17

Ephesians 5:21

~~~

As we got back into the car and headed to the airport, Brandon never spoke a word. Ava spent most of the time picking on me for whining about moving my arm. She was really all heart, and it was all an act, but she continued, "It's okay, baby, I will help you get back to your superhero status around our house."

As we boarded the plane, Brandon joined us. He would be continuing on to Miami to work on another case.

We were about an hour into our flight, and Ava was asleep. I was facing Brandon, who was in the seat across from mine. I was reading a book when Brandon looked up and asked me a question.

"Collin, I want to ask you something. If you can't answer it, I understand, but I am asking you anyway."

"Sure man. Go ahead. What is it?"

"I have seen a lot of evil in the world, and nothing gets me going more than squashing some guy like Henry. But how can you really worship a God who would let this kind of stuff happen—a God who lets kids get molested?"

The words were no more out of his mouth than I felt the vision coming as my mind penetrated the keyhole of a door and entered into a dark room. In the room was a small boy lying with his face down on one side of a pillow. His stare was one of fear and pain, as if he was waiting for something to happen at any moment.

Just then I heard the footsteps coming up the stairs, slow and heavy as they reached the top of the stairs. The knob on the door turned slowly, and a man entered the room. "I know you're not asleep, Brandon, and you know what time it is, right?" Silence came as the small boy shut his eyes in pain.

"Brandon, you don't want to make this hard, do you, son?" The man took his boots off and put them on the floor and then began to undress as he climbed into the bed next to the small boy. The boy kept his back to him as the man put his hand on his shoulder.

I wanted to scream, "Stop!" I wanted to save this young boy. I could imagine myself breaking into the room and grabbing the guy's head and slamming him to the floor. I wanted to rescue this little boy, but I couldn't. I could only watch as the boy finally spoke the words, "It hurts too much."

"I know," the man said, "but it will get easier. Just relax and enjoy it."

"Enjoy what?" I wanted to scream. Enjoy shooting you in the face if I could.

Just then a knock came to the door, and a women's voice spoke. "Carl, what are you doing? Brandon is not feeling well today. He needs time alone."

"Woman, you just go cook me some dinner. Me and Brandon are talking. I will be down in a minute."

"Carl, your dinner is ready. Come now," the voice came back with a stronger tone.

"Shut up and go downstairs. I'll come down when I'm ready."

Silence again filled the air, and then the haunting footsteps began to ring out as the woman retreated from the door and back down into the living area.

When the man was done, all I could see was the horror in the young boy's eyes as the door closed. Tears ran down his face as he prayed to God. "Please help me, God. I need You to make him stop. Please help me." He paused and then said, "Just let me die," as he shut his eyes to go to sleep.

I wasn't sure at whom I was more furious, the man, or the woman, or God for allowing it to happen. I quickly shunned the thought of being mad at God for I knew what I had seen was Satan at work, but the emotion nonetheless coursed through my mind.

As I came back, the adult Brandon had never skipped a beat and never noticed that I had drifted away for any amount of time.

He continued, "I listened to your messages, and I have been impressed with how you have handled yourself so far, but really,

Collin, what kind of God lets so many of his innocent children get hurt by these horrible people? I just don't get it."

I hesitated to answer him but said a quick prayer, asking God to answer him, not me. To be honest, I had no answers for him. Only embarrassment, remorse, and anger flowed through my mind.

Just then the scripture came to me. "Brandon, there is a scripture that says for the person who hurts one of God's children it would be better for him to have a large boulder tied around his neck and be thrown into the sea than it would be for him to face God's judgment for such acts. But we all have judgment coming, not just Henry and child molesters, but everyone, you and me included. Brandon, I admire your profession as you put your life on the line every day to keep us safe. But when you catch a guy and he goes to jail, sometimes it is years before he is ever brought to trial, correct?"

"That's right," Brandon replied.

"Well, it's the same way with God, Brandon. We like to judge God on what we think He is or what we want Him to be, but God says to judge Him based on who He says He is, not who we say He is. God is a loving Father, and He does care for us, but we live in a sinful world, and bad things happen to everybody, not just the deserving. This world is not the court. Court is not in session yet, and the reason is that all the parties are not accounted for. God will judge every person for his or her works one day. The reason Jesus is so important is His works are righteous, and He paid with His life for my sins and yours—for all sin.

"We are not much different from anyone else, Brandon, even from those people you arrest. The biggest difference is that what we think in our minds we don't necessarily do. But we are all self-righteous, pious, self-serving individuals, and without Christ living in us, the only goodness we show is nothing more than the goodness we believe ourselves to have. We are a world of self-worshiping souls who think we know better than the God who created everything, including us."

I then shut up, realizing I had been talking a lot and needed a break. Brandon just sat there with his eyes wide open, as if to say, "What in the world are you talking about, man? Are you crazy or what?"

A lifetime seemed to go by, and then Brandon finally said, "I guess I need to know more about this God you're talking about, because I had no idea He was all those things. I know I have my own issues, but I guess more than anything I have regret."

Then I said, "I know what that feels like—regret, I mean. Regret is something I have a hard time letting go of as well. Brandon, I know what happened when you were a boy, and I am so sorry for that."

"What do you mean, you know? What are you talking about?"

"I saw the man. I heard the steps. I know what he did."

"You need to shut up, Collin. You don't know anything about that."

His anger kindled quickly, and I realized maybe I should not have said anything, but it was too late to back off now, so I went full steam ahead. "I may not know what that was like exactly, but I hate the evil in this world. Brandon, he can't hurt you anymore, and there is a peace for you if you want it."

"Collin, who are you to see that in my life? That is none of your business. It's something no one knows but me and your supposedly great God."

"He is not just my God, Brandon. He is yours too."

"No, He is not. He may be your God, but He's not mine."

Silence was all that was left for the final hour of our flight. When we landed Brandon didn't say much. There was only a handshake and a hug from my wife as we departed from the plane.

I reminded Brandon that he had my cell phone number and that I would always be there for him and I hoped he would feel the same for me. He gave a pinch of a smile, and that was it as we walked to the terminal to finally go home.

What a trip this had been, certainly one I would not forget. Now I just wanted to rest and spend time with my family and friends again and get back to teaching and working in my community. Finally, we were back home, and I was so glad. I could not wait to see my beautiful family all back in the same house again. On the ride home, I held Ava's hand with my good arm and told her how much I loved her. She just smiled as if she knew, but I was glad I said it anyway.

When we arrived home, it was early in the morning, and the boys were still asleep. Ava's dad was up already making coffee and gave her a big smile when we entered the kitchen. He and the kids got back a couple of days prior to us and watched the boys until we returned. "Well, Collin, it looks like you have been a busy man. What's next for you? I wonder. Ava, you sure can pick 'em, sweetie," he said as he kissed her on her forehead.

"I know, Dad, but I think I am going to keep this one at least for a little while. Where are my angels, Dad?" she said as she hit me on my hurt arm. "I missed them so much."

I shrilled in pain, and she quickly apologized with a laugh. She hadn't meant to do it but didn't really feel that bad about it either.

We crept into the boys' room, and they were all asleep in the same bed. Ava lay down with them on one side and I on the other. We didn't have much room, but who cared? It was home again, and my heart was full.

We woke up an hour later with the boys beside themselves that we were all finally back together again.

The church was having a fall festival that evening with rides and games and just a great time for families and friends to get together. We were excited to get to see everyone again, and there was a lot going on that I needed to catch up on at work. I told Ava I would go early and meet her and the boys there in a little while.

I called Pastor Mike to see if he was going to be around so we could catch up. I got no answer, so I just left a voicemail and headed to the church. As I pulled up to the front building, I saw several luxury cars. That was not the norm, so it piqued my curiosity.

As I walked into the door and went to Mike's office, I could see the door was closed, so I peeked in the small window to see who was in there. As soon as I looked, four men, including Mike, looked back at me and smiled. It was embarrassing to say the least, as I felt like I was a snoop, but, well, maybe I was. Whatever the case, Mike opened the door, gave me a hug, and said, "Hey, brother, I missed you. Come on in. This has to do with you anyway."

As I entered the door, the other men stood up. I realized one was Dr. Russell from California, and we quickly smiled and embraced as we all sat down. The other two men were also from California and were meeting with Mike about doing the satellite church Dr. Russell and I—mostly Dr. Russell—had been working on. The idea had morphed into a team approach in regard to the services so that the televised program would be based not just on one pastor but on four of them. Each pastor would focus on his specialty and gifts. The program would air once a week with a different pastor every week for the four weeks.

Mike began, "Collin, we really need you to help with this, and we hope you will pray about it. This program will be called *The Truth* and will not just be about one pastor or even one organization. This program will be in place specifically to develop missionaries across our nation first and then the world.

"It will include news segments with live feeds to mission projects we are doing. It will include a discipleship support line, as well as support for the unsaved. God is using us to produce a new generation of Christians, a generation of followers who will work together, not for religion but for His glory and that alone. I realize this is lot to take in, but please let us know, first, if you would be a part of this and, second, if you would be one of the main four to provide us with the messages each month."

I went home just before the harvest festival was to start to get a quick shower and head back to the church. Ava and the boys had already left to help set up, so I was all alone in the house. The silence was actually pleasant, but I realized quickly how much I loved my family. With all the business and events that had been occurring over the past several years, I realized something that day that has stayed with me since. While taking a shower with only the sound of the water running and a dog barking outside at who knows what, I realized none of this mattered without my family being there.

I knew the importance of God being the head of my life and all things, but the blessedness of my family is what mattered on this earth. I understood that regardless of money or possessions or any fame that could come from a TV show or a book, it was my family that gave me joy, and it was my servant hood to Christ that I valued. I had a sudden burden on my heart for those without a family, those people wandering around just trying to survive by themselves.

What a sadness it would be to be alone without loved ones, not to even mention not having Christ. I thought of Ava and me and our family and how we would make it our life's mission to bring the joy of family to as many others as possible. I sank my head down as the water drained down my back. I was in awe of who God is and of His desire to have me in His family. He calls me His child, a child of a king.

Chapter 18

Luke 5:32

When I arrived at the festival that evening, I could smell the hot dogs cooking. The sun was just going down, and the lights from the event were mixing with it as if it was all designed to happen that way.

People were laughing, but it was the children's voices I could hear the most, as they played games outside. I have come to realize that these are the memories I enjoy the most—memories of simplistic, basic, wonderful events. Yet many times we just let them slip by, focusing on things that may never even happen. We focus our lives on things like jobs we have or don't have or an event that has built up expectations in our minds that will never be met. But these actual moments are what make the real difference, and they are what we are to enjoy.

As I was thinking on this very thing, my mind quickly shifted back to my desire to get Ava alone to talk about the job offer and what God had laid on my heart about adopting. You see what I mean? That's exactly it. I was enjoying the moment, and then I stole it from myself, thinking about things that aren't even here yet.

Just then I looked up and saw Ava holding our little baby Cooper and laughing at Spencer and Michael (Scooter). I just wanted to enjoy this time with them; the rest could wait.

I approached Michael and said, "Hey, buddy, how you doing?"

He smiled with those braces shining bright and said, "I'm good, Dad. Glad you're back."

I realized how quickly he had grown in such a little time. He was in ninth grade and just a little taller than I was. His had nickname stayed with him through the years, and I think he liked it. It was funny how many people never even asked him what his real name was.

As we were talking, I felt something pounce on my back, and my knees buckled a little under the pressure. It was Spencer, who I quickly realized had been growing as well. He had had the sudden impulse to to ride me like a donkey.

I laughed as I almost fell, and he jumped off, knowing he was bigger than we both realized—not fat, just becoming a man. I held Ava's hand as we walked around that night, listening to music and enjoying a life I didn't deserve but gladly accepted.

As things were wrapping up, I couldn't help but think of Brandon and Henry and the circumstances that surrounded both their lives. As different as they both were, I made it a point that I was going to write both of them a letter as soon as I had a moment to catch up. In some way I wanted to help both of them carry their burdens, much more Brandon than Henry, especially since Brandon was the one who didn't want me dead.

We drove home that night, and as we walked in the door, I noticed the answering machine blinking as usual. I have to say, the excitement from all the press, the questions, interviews, and shows, as well as all the conversations, was losing its luster quickly. I looked at Ava before she pushed the button and said, "Baby, not tonight, okay?"

She laughed and said, "Amen, big boy." Then she raised one hand in the air and put out a "woop, woop."

The kids died laughing, even Scooter, who was at that age of trying to be a little cooler on the outside than he was on the inside.

Anyway, Ava really knew how to talk to them better than I, and she didn't care what they thought about how she acted. She was also quick to tell them that I was her partner, and as much as she loved them, I was important too—even more so since I was going to be around after they had left home. I think they respected her all the more for that stand. They knew she loved them, and she showed it every day, but for her to honor me with those words meant a lot to me, more than she would ever know.

As she walked them up the stairs, she said, "All right, boys, it's time for bed. Daddy and I are going to have some alone time. Ohhh yeah, you know, some kissing time."

"Gross!" Spencer yelled out, as we all laughed. I just collapsed on the couch and turned on the TV, which I had not touched in forever. Ava got Cooper to sleep and joined me about thirty minutes later.

I was flipping through the channels, moving quickly toward the sports channel when I saw my picture flash up on the screen. I stopped and turned the volume up. The picture was of Henry and me. Apparently, Henry had taken his own life in jail by hanging himself with some linen he had taken from the laundry of the prison. Ava sat down just as the news went off and said, "What was that all about?" I told her what I had just heard, and we both just sat there trying to soak it all in.

As we lay there, the question kept going through my mind: How does a soul that has claimed the freedom of Christ become so enslaved in something, as Henry had? How does a soul get so lost in its own mission that it becomes a slave to itself and not to the freedom it once tasted? My wife quickly reminded me that that is exactly what happened to the Pharisees in the Bible. They were students of the law, but they took the laws of God and made them into something they were never supposed to be. They didn't want a man's hand to be healed on the Sabbath because it would be a work, and work was not to be done on that day. Jesus had to remind them that God made the Sabbath to serve man, not man to serve the Sabbath.

It is like that with all the laws of God. God established the laws to help us, not hurt us. He made them to protect us and to show us that He is the Holy Father and Creator who detests sin and disobedience.

I preached freedom from our sins through the sacrifice of Jesus, and Henry could not accept that. He could not accept that in Christ we are free from our sins.

Again, Ava reminded me that Jesus said to follow Him, for His yoke is easy and His burden is light. To Henry that burden was heavy, and he had to carry it, not only by obeying the law out of duty but also by stopping anyone from saying anything contrary.

My heart went out to him, but more so I realized that Jesus paid a heavy price for my sins and freeing me from them. This reminded me that now I followed Him out of love for Him and out of gratitude for salvation, not out of duty.

The verse that came to my mind and put me at rest was John 14:15: "If [you] love me, keep my commandments." I had always thought this verse was saying I had to prove my love to Him through keeping His commandments. But what it really says is if I love Him, I will *want* to keep His commandments. I prayed that night that my love for Him would continue to grow so that my obedience would be a reflection of my love, not my works.

Ava and I spent some time on the couch, which meant I rubbed her feet for an hour or so. We lay there just resting, not thinking about anything or even really talking, just resting in one another. We both fell asleep on the couch, and it was the best sleep I had had in a very long time.

The next day, after a great breakfast and some well overdue cleaning around the house, we received a letter, and it was marked from the prison Henry had been in. It read as follows:

Collin,

I am sure you know by now what I have done. I wanted to send you this letter so that you understand why I did what I did. I cannot live in this world any longer, for it has nothing for me. I know you probably think I am insane for doing what I did, but I believe what you are doing is wrong, and I thought I could stop it. You tell people they have a choice and you preach freedom, but I have never known that to be true. We are all under God's control, and we do only what He devises we do in His will. There is no freedom, only judgment. I will be facing that judgment soon, just as one day you will too. I have served God, and I will be judged for that and rewarded for all I have obeyed. You will be judged for your actions, and they will surely bring you to your demise. I die, knowing I did what the Lord had planned and that nothing is accomplished apart from His will.

Henry

As I read this letter, I couldn't believe a person could have so much confidence in something that was so wrong. Henry really believed that God wanted him to try to kill me and that God's will was for him to kill himself. How sad it was to know that Henry died believing that message of imprisonment and that someday he would be rewarded for his merit in this life—rewarded and judged for obeying and not surrendering.

The Bible says that the only thing good in us is Christ. Our very best works are as filthy rags before God. I felt compassion for Henry, for I realized how much error his father had instilled in him.

As I finished the letter, I felt like a chapter had ended in my life, and I must say, I was actually looking forward to a new one.

Monday morning came early, and I felt an urge to go running; so I got up, put on my workout shorts and a hoodie, and headed out the door. It was still dark, but I had my bright yellow running shoes on, so at least early morning commuters could see some part of me.

As I started the run, I could feel the wind on my head and face. It was just a slight breeze, but it felt amazing. I loved to run, but it just didn't seem like there was enough time in the day to get it in. I felt my bones trying to adapt to my pace, and it wasn't working so well, for the moment anyway.

I had my headset on, so I turned up the music to help take my mind off my breathing and maybe get some adrenaline going. To be honest, I wondered if I had any left.

I had my hoodie over my head as I was turned back into my neighborhood to finish my run. One of my favorite songs was playing, and I really wasn't paying much attention to anything around me. But as

I turned into the entrance, I caught something out of the corner of my eye.

It was a woman with a dog. The dog was much bigger than the lady, and that's never a good combination when you're the one on the other side of the leash.

As I squared off with them both, the dog looked up, and I realized what I was dealing with: a mastiff. Mastiff—what a name! It seems like a fitting name for a dog that size. We were almost looking eye to eye—another combination that did not sit in my favor. The dog came charging at me. The little woman on the other end of that leash was like a rag doll being pulled along by the strength of this beast.

That adrenaline I thought I had lost suddenly reappeared, so apparently I had at least a little left. I quickly used it to run far away from both the lady and the dog. Luckily, that was enough for this dog, and he stopped trying to attack me.

When I was far enough away to know I had escaped, I felt the Holy Spirit speaking to me. He said, "Collin that is what I am supposed to be like in you. I am to be a mastiff, not a chihuahua. When Satan and his demons come to attack, I should be that powerful force that turns them back."

What a revelation, I thought. What I would give for that to be true. I understood, and I wanted to make that happen. It was not about the Holy Spirit being able to do this but about me allowing it to be this way. I vowed to spend more time praying and studying the Word of God, for I wanted this to be true for me and not just a hope.

When I got home, I had a few hours before I had to be at the church and get back to work, so I decided to make Ava and the boys some breakfast and take the baby so Ava could get a little more sleep.

Cooper had a diaper full and wanted me to know it. That was my first task, and I was not looking forward to opening that package. Ava gladly took me up on the offer and laid her head back down on the pillow. I figured I should get some praise for this or at least an award, but Ava didn't have the same enthusiasm I did about my doing this great work.

I realize, of course, she did this every day, so for me to pick up these duties, however noble it was, did not cause her to make it that great of a deal.

I fed the boys, and off to school they went. Cooper was ready to take a nap, so I put him in bed with Ava. "I gotta get ready for work, so he's all yours, baby," I said.

Ava laughed as I dumped him onto her and quickly got into the shower and ready to leave. As I was leaving, she pulled me close to her and kissed me softly on the neck and said, "Thanks, baby, for the extra sleep. I love you this much." She held her thumb and index finger almost together. I felt my body go limp as her lips touched my neck. It was as if she had some power over me.

Just as quickly as I had lost reality for that brief moment, she quickly gave me a smack on the cheek and said, "Now go bring home the bacon, big boy. See you later, if you know what I mean."

I did know what she meant, and it certainly gave me something to look forward to that day. It really doesn't matter how good or bad the day is when you know you have a woman like that to come home to and she actually wants you to come home.

I got to the office and received a text from Ava saying she was taking Cooper shopping to get the boys some shoes and she would bring me some lunch around noon. I texted her back to say that sounded great, and then I began my day.

I began catching up on my e-mails as well as really trying to think through this new proposition of a four-leader, nationwide discipleship church. I knew what an opportunity this was, for the other three men were great leaders. In fact, I felt underqualified to work with them. I was like a sponge around them, though, and they had more confidence in me than I did, so I thought, Why not? It all seemed to fit, but just before I sent the e-mail out to say yes, my phone rang.

"Mr. Keith, this is Officer Rob Canon. I need to let you know your wife and child have been in an accident and you need to meet me at the ER at Regional as soon as you can. Please have someone bring you."

I'm not sure what I screamed, but the officer said, "Mr. Keith, please calm down."

"Are they all right?" I shouted back.

"Sir, I need you to come here now, and please calm down. That's why you need another driver. They are working on them now."

I hung up the phone and ran to Mike's office. I burst through the door and said, "Mike, they have been in an accident. Please pray for them."

"Who?" Mike replied, as I ran down the hall.

"Ava and Cooper."

I rushed through the door to the outside so hard it sounded as if I had broken it. I felt the adrenalin rushing to my head as I jumped into my car and started the engine. I didn't care what the policeman had said about getting a driver. I knew no one would get me there faster than I would.

Then I realized what I had told Mike to do is what I really needed to do, so I did. It was a violent prayer, as I pleaded with God to help them.

"Please, God, I can't take this. I can't live without her, God. Cooper is just a baby, God. He hasn't even had a chance to live. Please, God, take me, not them."

I then started to just speak goodness into the air: "They are going to be fine, God. I believe You will bring them out of this. God, I know You are all-powerful and nothing is out of Your control. They are in Your hands."

I pulled up to the ER, parked on the curb, and ran through the glass door. The officer was waiting and quickly put his hands up. "Mr. Keith, you have got to calm down now."

"Calm down for what?" I barked back. "Are they okay?"

"No, Mr. Keith, they are not. I need you—they need you—to get your senses back. They need you to be there for them right now."

I breathed in deeply, as if it were the first time I had taken a breath since he had called me. My lip was quivering as I exhaled.

The officer quickly said, "Good. Now follow me."

He took me to a room I was all too familiar with. It was a room where you are put to wait for the doctor to come and give you news no one wants to hear and the pain cannot be heard by others.

I sat down in the room, and the officer said he was going to get the doctor. I quickly got on my knees and started to pray again that God would save them from whatever this was.

I heard the door open, but instead of the doctor, it was Mike. He grabbed my shoulders and said, "Collin, we are going to get through this."

"Get through what? Do you know what's happened?"

"No, I don't, but let's sit right here and pray until they tell us, okay?" We sat down, and I felt the tears flowing from my eyes as he prayed. I didn't even hear what he was saying, for I was denying to my very soul that this was happening right now. We had been through too much, and I was tired of fighting.

Just then the door opened, and I saw a man towering above me. He was at least six feet four, and he did not say a word. I knew at that moment what had happened. It was as if my soul sank away. My knees got weak, and that's all I remember.

I woke up some time later on a hospital bed feeling sedated. Mike was standing over me, holding my hand. "What is going on, Mike? What happened?"

"Collin, I am so sorry, but they are gone."

"No! Don't tell me that! That's not true!" I lifted myself up, but Mike grabbed my shoulder.

"Collin, listen to me, you have two boys who are going to be getting out of school in about an hour, and they need you to be strong. You are the only one who can do this for them, and they are going to be depending on you for help."

As I lay back on the bed, I knew he was right. I sat there as Mike told me the entire story the officer had told him. He said that a young man and three of his friends had ditched school that day and were riding around; he believed they were texting but was not sure yet whether drugs or alcohol was involved. None of them was seriously injured because they were in a much larger vehicle. It crossed over into the other lane and hit Ava and Cooper's car head-on.

"Collin, the doctor spoke up, "even with the safety belts, the impact was so severe they didn't have a chance. I just wanted you to know. I don't think they felt much pain."

Believe it or not, as hurt and angry as I was, the idea of it happening quickly and them feeling no pain gave me the slightest comfort. But even the slightest bit was like a cup of water to a man dying of thirst.

"I just can't believe this happened, Mike. It's not right. That should have been me, not them. She is the one who holds everything together. She is my everything, and Cooper didn't even get a chance to live his life."

Mike stopped me abruptly, and although he didn't smack me in the face, his words felt the same. It was an awakening that continues to echo in my mind as I live without Ava and Cooper to this day.

Mike said almost in a yell, "Collin, you listen to me. She is not everything; she is not what holds your life together, and you know it. Do not put that on her. That is Jesus' responsibility, and you must not give that to her. Ava and Cooper are gone, but He is not. This is life, Collin, and you know it. It's not fair for anybody. This is your cross. Will you carry it, or will you give up? Would Ava have given up?"

The shock of his words washed over me, and my mind received them at the same time my spirit did. At that second, I felt the rush of acceptance flow over me as if it were a tidal wave. All I could say as I fell on his shoulders was, "I miss hear already so much."

We didn't speak for minutes. We just sat there in the silence of the room. I knew he was right, and in a short, silent prayer, I said, "Jesus, I am Yours. Please help me."

I felt the strength come back into my core, and I slowly stood up. "Let's go pick up Scooter and Spencer. I don't want them finding out without me there."

"Are you sure, Collin?" Mike asked.

"Yes," I replied. There was no way they were going to hear this from anyone but me.

As we left the hospital, I still couldn't help but wish some miracle would happen and the doctors would call me to say they had miraculously come back to life. I knew in my heart, though, they were gone, along with a part of me. They would remain only in my heart and mind.

We arrived at the school, and the principal, who had already been notified, met us in the parking lot. She had tears in her eyes as she approached us but was fighting through it. "Collin, I am so sorry," she said. "I have not pulled the boys out of class yet, but I was going to before the final bell rang if you weren't here yet. I want you to come to my office, and I will have them come in, okay?" I nodded as we entered her office.

As I sat down, my eyes focused on all the pictures in her office, pictures of her kids and husband at different places. There were goofy pictures and a few family ones, the kind you get dressed up for. I couldn't help but reflect on how similar she and Ava were when it came to being a mom.

The happiness on the faces in the pictures was real and not scripted. It was as if they had been caught in a perfect moment of joy. We had the same kind of pictures all around our house, and I wondered if we would have any more of those days ahead of us. I told my heart at that very moment we would, and I believe that was the moment I decided to fight. I would not let this be the end of Ava and Cooper.

As my mind centered on this thought, the door opened, and both boys came into the office with eyes wide open. They seemed relieved when they saw me, and almost in a whisper both said, "Hey, Dad. What's going on?" Scooter continued, "Why did the security guard bring me to Spencer's school? Did he do something wrong again?"

I wanted to laugh at his remark, and a chuckle came out as I said, "No, son." I wondered how I could even have a laugh in me, but the sight of my boys, my remaining family, gave me more hope than despair.

As we sat down, the idea of how much this was going to hurt them was piercing my brain like nails. I wasn't sure I could speak the words. I wanted to be strong, but I could not open my mouth. Just then another knock came to the door. It was Ava's dad. I had never even called him, but Mike had, and I was glad he did as my father-in-law walked in and sat down.

He had a grey beard now, and since his wife had died, he had been even closer to Ava and the boys and me. The boys loved him. He was a great granddad, and I actually envied him in many ways. He seemed to be cut from a different fabric than most, tougher, almost impenetrable, if you know what I mean. He was calm and cool in almost every way, and his very presence brought a since of peace to the room.

Scooter again said, "Dad, what is going on? Why won't you tell us? Why is everyone here?"

Poppy looked at me with those confident eyes and nodded as if to say, "This is why you're the dad. Do your job, son."

My mouth opened and strength came from somewhere within me. "Boys, it's about your mom and Cooper. Earlier today they had a car accident; it was a really bad accident. Boys, your mom and Cooper are not with us anymore. The doctors couldn't bring them back. I am so sorry."

Michael's eyes got big as saucers, and I felt his breath go away, as if someone had kicked him in the stomach. "What, Dad? Please, say no. Please, Dad, don't say that."

Spencer ran to my arms and hugged me as tight as he could. He didn't say anything. He didn't have to. I could feel the helplessness in his small frame.

Michael hung his head with his hands over his face and didn't speak again. As we walked to the car, Poppy asked if he could drive Michael home. He wanted to talk to him for a little while.

"Sure," I said. I believe Michael welcomed his strength. They both got into his truck and left. I took Spencer to the house, and Mike stayed with us that entire day.

Poppy and Scooter didn't speak for a long time. The road they took was unfamiliar and long. Finally, Michael looked at his grandfather and asked, "Where are we going, Poppy?"

"It's a place that is very special to me. We will be there in a minute." They turned off the main road onto a dirt one that wound all the way down to a creek and what looked like an old swing. They both got out of the truck, and Poppy walked over to a tree that had a carving in it. There were initials still etched into

the tree. Michael didn't really know what it was.

Poppy spoke up and said, "This is where I took your grandma on our first date. We came out here. She had made us a lunch, and we sat here by this old swing, and I realized that day God had given me someone very special to spend my life with.

"We etched our names on this old tree some time later so that we would not forget where it all started. Every year it seemed we would try to come back here to talk about all the joy God gave us. Sometimes we wouldn't say anything because our hearts were filled and nothing needed to be said. We would just sit here and remember."

So, what's the other initials below yours and Grandma's?

Poppy slowly turned to Michael and said, "That's your mama's initials, son. God blessed me with two of the most wonderful women in the world, and this is my place for remembering them. I am hurting too, and it's going to get worse before it gets better. But always remember this, Scooter, God makes Himself known through our suffering, and that is when He is the closest, not the furthest away.

"You find your place, son, where you can remember all the joy your mom brought to you, and you fight, son, you fight. We have to be strong through this. Your brother is watching you, and as strong

Luke 5:32

as your dad is, he needs you now more than ever." With that said, Poppy just sat there as the sun went down, and Michael seemed to find a little peace in the midst of an overwhelming sorrow.

By the time Michael got back, many people had already shown up and left. A few had stayed, and I could tell the boys were exhausted. I thanked those who were still there for their time and told them we just needed some time to be alone. As they all left and it was just us in the house, it felt like our home was missing the one thing that made it a home. We all fell asleep on the couch that night. I don't believe any of us cared about tomorrow. We were numb to this world, even if just for a moment.

Chapter 19

Psalm 6:1-9

The days following the loss of Ava and Cooper were filled with many piercing and painful moments, but not all were sad. There were times of blissful memories that would cause me to smile, and then more pain came rushing in as I realized there were no more of those memories to come here in this world. The idea of seeing them again in heaven, as pleasing as it is, didn't give me the comfort I hoped it would.

I wanted our time back, time to spend together as a family. I felt the bitterness coursing through my veins, and I wanted it to stop, but it would not.

The funeral was beautiful and horrible all at the same time. So many people came with love and support. There was a beautiful large casket and one small one and many beautiful flowers. Yet *beautiful* seemed to be the wrong word for this. Nothing about this was beautiful because it was my family, not someone else's.

Psalm 6:1-9

This was my wife and child, and all the love and support and all the arrangements and sweet words of prayer and advice just made me even angrier that they were gone. As I sat at the funeral that day, I looked over at my two boys with tears rolling down their eyes, and I understood that with this one event my boys lost their innocence forever. Because of this they had to become men before their time.

After the funeral we went home. Poppy also came for a much-needed rest. I did not know what was next for me, but it suddenly hit me that while everyone was praying for me, I had not been praying at all. I had not talked to God much at all lately. Maybe I was mad at Him, but I had not done it on purpose. I finally got on my knees that night, but I never said a word. I just listened.

What I heard was the silence of a Father who seemed like He had gone away—no angels, no signs, just silence. I climbed into my bed, never doubting God existed but wondering how much He cared. As I lay in the darkness, it seemed like even my bed had abandoned me. The silence of the room was so loud I held my hands over my ears. It was the strangest thing. The silence in that room that night was louder than anything I had ever heard. I couldn't sleep, and I didn't want to pray. I didn't even want to watch the TV. What I really wanted was to just die. I just wanted it all to end—no more interviews, no more loneliness, no more responsibilities. I just wanted to be somewhere else, not here without Ava. As I lay there, I looked out the window and suddenly remembered how many times before I had done the same thing as I was growing up. I looked over into the other window, where I used to see Ava, and I remembered how we talked to one another and laughed with each other from those windows. That window in my house was a window to my past, and until that moment I never understood the importance of it. I lay there for at least an hour, peacefully remembering the many times we shared from window to window.

Finally, I drifted off to sleep and began to dream. I knew I was asleep, yet it seemed so real. I was at the pond down from the house. Two kids were swinging with a woman standing in front and between them, pushing them back as they glided back on the swings. As I came closer and closer, their laughter became contagious, and I started to feel myself smile as I heard their sweet voices. As I came even closer, the woman looked over her shoulder and smiled. As soon as she turned, I stopped breathing, as I realized it was Ava.

Oh, she was so unbelievably stunning. She wore a white, cotton sundress that came down to her knees. The breeze made her long, auburn hair sway a little to the side. She looked at me with eyes that were greener than I had ever remembered. She left the kids and began to walk toward me. I stopped as she came ever so close. She softly kissed me on my lips, and my whole body trembled. I felt my knees give, and I fell to the ground on them. She gently lowered to where I was and put her hands on the sides of my face. I knew I was dreaming and the dream would come to an end, so I said, "I don't want to leave, Ava. I miss you too much."

She smiled and then turned and pointed and said, "Look, it's Cooper and Scotty."

As I looked I saw Cooper was off the swing and almost to us. My eyes widened as he approached and said, "Hey, Daddy I miss you." His little arms wrapped around my neck. He wasn't sad, though; he was happy. He then turned and said, "Look, Daddy, it's Scotty."

I didn't understand it at first, but then the little boy put his hand in mine and said, "Hey, Daddy. I love you." As soon as he said "Daddy," I realized this was Cooper's twin, who never made it: Anthony Scott. He was so perfect. He had blonde hair and a curious smile that made his eyes almost close. "We love you so much, Daddy. Please don't be sad anymore." With that they ran back to the swings, giggling and grabbing one another to see who would make it there first.

Ava looked at me and, with her voice in perfect harmony with my soul, said, "Collin, God is not done with you, baby. He has more for you to do, and Spencer and Michael need you to be strong. I am always with you. Don't you see I am more than just a dream, more than even the life we shared. I am always yours, baby. You can't give up. I am going now, but remember we are always going to love you and we will never leave you. All you have to do is look for us in all the places you know we are."

I woke in my bedroom and quickly turned on the lamp on the nightstand. I took in a huge breath, as if life were being sucked into my lungs for the first time. I missed her so much, but now the house and the bed were the way they were before. I leaned back in solace, knowing that even though she had left and would not be with us physically, we could still feel her presence spiritually.

It was my doubt and disbelief and my pride that brought me loneliness. She was there all along. What I most remember is that when I woke I could smell her sweet scent. It lingered on all that she had, it seemed. I went to the closet and pulled out her favorite dress and put it to my nose. I smelled it as if it were a flower, and her aroma filled my senses.

The next morning was a Saturday, and I got up and made everyone breakfast. It was what we used to do when Ava and Cooper were with us, and to me they were back. Scooter came down first and stumbled into the kitchen seemingly surprised I was cooking.

"What's up, Dad? Making breakfast, huh?"

"Yep. You want some pancakes to go along with the rest?"

"Yeah, that would be great," he replied as he came behind me and hugged me around the shoulders. "I love ya, Dad."

"I love you too. We're going to be all right, you know."

"Yeah, I just miss her."

"Me too. I think what I am going to do, son, is keep doing what we have always done as a family, and in that I think in some way they will always be a part of it."

"That sounds good to me."

"You want to go to the flea market today and see what's up on some fishing gear?"

"Absolutely, and I think Poppy would like that too."

As we sat there that morning, I realized that Scooter, now nearly sixteen, was a man, and I figured I was going to start calling him Michael from then on. Scooter would be for everybody else.

"How is school going?"

"It's okay. I am ready to graduate, though. I am thinking about getting a job too."

"Where at?"

"I don't know. Maybe the grocery store or Academy Sports would be okay."

I could see in his eyes he would prefer Academy Sports, and I knew the manager there, so I mentally filed that on the to-do list for the upcoming week.

As Michael got up and went to the fridge for more orange juice, I felt my mind go off. This was the first time this had happened in at least a week. It was a clear image of Michael and a friend of his walking down the hall at school. It was as if I were walking behind them but close enough to hear and see everything through his eyes. I saw a girl looking at Michael and smiling and then another. It was apparent how attractive he had become to the opposite sex. Conner, his friend, noticed as well and said, "That's a cute little honey. You should hook up with that one, big boy."

"She is cute," Michael replied, "but I ain't sleeping with none of these girls. You know my deal."

"Yeah, I know, your marriage bond. But what if you get married, and she ain't no good? Then you're stuck."

"Well, I guess I would rather be stuck than end up with some STD like you're going to have, or already have, if you don't stop."

"What's that, you jerk? Don't be wishing bad luck on me. I ain't sleeping with no sluts."

"Yeah, I know. You're the only one they have slept with, I'm sure. You're so special."

"Scooter, you got to loosen up, man. Have some fun. You deserve it with all you've been through, man. Let's double-date next weekend. I will get the girls, and I got a joint from my brother, so let's have some fun for once."

Michael stopped and turned so Conner could see his eyes. "Conner, listen to me. That's not who I am, and if that's what you want me to be, then I'm sorry; it's not going to happen. You're the one who needs to learn to have fun. I don't need that crap anyway, and when did you start needing it? What's up with you lately, man? You're asking about me, but what's with you? Are you okay?" They began to walk again.

"I am great," Conner said. "Beside the fact that my dad's a jerk and my mom is always working, I am fantastic. Don't make this about me, Scooter. You're the one who needs to relax."

"Whatever, brother. I am here for you if you need me, but I am not going down that road with you."

"Whatever, yourself," Conner said as they split up.

I came quickly back to the present as Michael sat back down. I was so proud of him I couldn't even speak really. I just said, "Son, you're awesome, you know that?"

"Thanks, Dad, but I am not sure what you mean."

"I am just proud of you, and one day you're going to make some girl really happy."

"You think? I'm not so sure about that. The girls I know don't seem to wait on much, and they go after the rebels, not guys like me."

"You're right, but that's no different from when I was growing up. Young girls are stupid too, you know. It's not just the guys at your age. They get caught up in the idea that freedom is something rebellious. They will find out just as my generation and the generation before did that freedom is the last thing you get from living that way."

"Well, Dad, it's a whole lot easier to talk about it than it is to live it."

"I agree, but keep looking into the future, not the present mind-set. The best girls are the ones who have saved themselves. Those girls will soon be looking for their guy, and it won't be the rebel who likes to party; it will be the rebel who is strong enough to live his own life, not everyone else's. Trust me on this, son. Don't give up."

"I won't," he replied. "I miss mom so much, I guess I feel that if I live honorably, it will be my way of honoring her."

Silence filled the room after he said those words because I was speechless. Minutes passed as I finished cooking. Then, before Michael went up to wake Spencer, I said, "Son, your mother loved you more than anything in this life, and no matter what happens and no matter what mistakes you make, the honor was always hers because she shared her life with you."

After breakfast we all showered and took off to the flea market. It was

a bright day, and there were a ton of people there. I looked down at my phone and

saw that I had missed a call. It was from Brandon. I tried to hear the message, but it was too noisy, so I decided to just listen to it later.

We spent a few hours going up and down the aisles of this place. If you ever want to watch people, this is the place, no doubt. Bikers, businessmen, blue collar, white collar, dirty collar, every race, creed, and nationality were at this place. We left around noon and stopped to get a burger at the Beacon Drive-in.

As we sat there, I looked again at my phone and saw that Brandon had left me another message. I stepped away and just returned the call instead of listening. It was only one ring before he picked up. I could immediately hear the energy in his voice. "Hey, Collin, how are you, man?"

"I am good, and who is this?" I said. "It can't be Brandon, at least not the one I know."

"It is, and I am glad you can tell a difference in me, brother, because there is."

"What's that?" I asked.

Brandon began to tell me that after he left from our last meeting, he began to talk to God. He began asking him for answers and searching for peace in all he had been through and seen.

He said, "First, Collin, I would get little signs, like people asking me how I was and people just more or less caring for me. Then a complete stranger asked me to come to church with him. I went, and after being there a month or so, I gave my heart to Christ, Collin. I really did it. And on top of all that, I met someone, and I think she is the one. Anyway I have so much to tell you. We are coming through tomorrow, and I want to introduce her to you and Ava."

I didn't have the heart to tell him yet since he was so happy, so I said, "Sure, brother. I am looking forward to it. See ya then."

I had no more than hung up and was heading back to my table when I saw across the way a man sitting by himself, eating. I could see who it was, and I wasn't sure how to feel. It was Mici, of all people, Michael's biological dad. He was about midway through his meal. I sat there and watched as we ate to see if he would ever look at us, but he never did. He just sat there, keeping to himself in silence. I saw that Poppy had noticed too, but we both continued to eat without saying anything. Spencer wanted ice cream when we finished, so I said I would go get it.

When I came back I saw that Poppy was gone, and I looked directly over to Mici's table to see him sitting there talking to him. I was shocked and wanted to go over, but I knew this moment was not about me, so I just sat there wondering what was being said.

I also realized I was still not over what he had done to Ava, and now that she was gone, it was even easier to hate him. I reminded myself of his struggle in the courtroom, but it didn't put out the flame of hate that still burned within. I really couldn't believe Poppy was even speaking to him. As we finished, I looked over again to see what was going on, and Poppy was heading back over to us. We got back into the truck and left, and I never asked what was said. I figured he would let me know if he wanted to.

Brandon got to the house the next evening about six, and we all sat down in the living room. The young woman he had brought with him was lovely in beauty and personality, and Brandon seemed to be walking on cloud nine. Her name was Eva, and I could tell she had a passion for Christ and for Brandon. Brandon immediately began to ask about Ava, and reluctantly I had to tell the story again.

I finally said, "Guys, I just don't want to talk about this anymore." Eva was in tears, and Brandon was without words. He finally just hugged me and said, "I am so sorry, brother. Please know we are here for you anytime, night or day."

They left that night and said they would see me at church the next day, and I watched them drive off. As much as I liked them both, I could feel jealousy overcome me for what they had that I didn't.

I sat back on the couch that evening and just reminisced about seeing Ava and my boys in that dream. I have to admit that after the dream I felt her presence more, and I had peace, but still the longing to be with her was tremendous. And at the end of the day, to be perfectly honest, I really didn't care much for this life without her in it.

Chapter 20
The Beginning of the End
Job 1:21

As the boys and I walked into church the next morning, many eyes were on us, as Ava's and Cooper's deaths were still the topic of discussion. The pastor had asked me if I would say something that morning, but I could not yet. I wasn't ready to speak in public about Ava and my child passing. As the opening music ended, I must admit it was powerful, and I felt the Sprit moving my heart. I was fighting hard not to break, and I sat down as soon as I had the opportunity. When the worship leader finished giving the announcements, he called Poppy up to speak, and it caught me off guard. As Ava's father approached the pulpit, I grew uneasy to say the least. He had spoken in church before on Veterans Day and on other occasions honoring the military since he was retired from the Marine Corps. This was not one of those occasions, and I wanted to avoid dealing with my wife's death entirely.

The Beginning of the End / Job 1:21

As he stood before the crowd, he was unshaken and direct. I am not sure if it was part of his training or if it was in his blood, but he was immovable in stature, like a rock that could not be shaken. He spoke directly and clearly but with a comforting tone that made you feel good he was on your side. He began, "For a Christian forgiveness is not a choice; it is a duty. It is no different than a marine dutifully choosing to give his life for his brother in the heat of battle. We think because we are in America we have the freedom to choose this or that. But that is the exact opposite of what true freedom is. True freedom is when nothing binds you and you can act in such a way as to honor those who sacrificed before you. Is it really freedom to eat foods that destroy your body or smoke things that sicken your lungs? Is it really freedom to take drugs that you grow dependent on and actually imprison you? Freedom is not just making choices; it is making the right choices. God is over all, and there is no freedom under Him, only in Him. That's what the beatitudes are about, which Jesus spoke to so many. Freedom is being in the Father and the Father in you. Freedom is the sacrifice Jesus, the greatest Leader the world has ever known, made when He gave His one and only life for everyone else. He gave it whether they asked for it or not.

"There are people in my life I have hated—hated because they took something away from someone I loved. I am not free because I choose to forgive or not forgive them; I am free only by forgiving them. Today to the world my daughter is dead because her body lies in the ground. I tell you today my daughter is free because she is with

Christ, and as selfish as I am and as much as I want her here with me, I realize she lived her life in such a way that this very moment would be her greatest moment.

"My daughter lived free because she forgave and loved people who hurt her. Do you hear me? She didn't just forgive them, but she also loved those who hurt her, and that is real freedom. She was free because she served her husband, family, and friends with kindness and sincerity and with the sweat of her brow. She was free and is free today because she lived for Another, for One, and that One is Jesus Christ. My daughter knew what freedom was, and I have learned that freedom through her life. Today I choose freedom, and I chose that by forgiving all. I choose to be a light and not a hindrance. I choose freedom. I choose to live for my brother, not to die with hate."

As he finished there was only silence, until one man stood up and walked down to the front. It was Mici, and he was obviously in need of forgiveness. I could not stop my emotions. Anger, hate, and love all battled to see which would win out in this moment. I realized everything Ava's dad had said was right, and I knew what I had to do. I stepped out in fear, not knowing what was going to happen, but I knew it was right, and I knew I was going to do it. In spite of all the emotions, I was going to choose good. As I came up behind him at the front of the church, Mici realized it was me. He said just three words as his knees hit the floor: "Please forgive me."

I knelt down with him, and as the words came out of my mouth, assuring him of my forgiveness, I understood what true freedom feels like.

I arrived home that evening with a new walk and a new vision for my life, I would forgive not only Mici but myself, not only those boys that ran into my wife and son but my past mistakes. I decided that I would not use Ava's and Cooper's death as a reason to be mad at God.

As I laid my head down and felt the rest poor over me I heard a knock on the door and almost decided to let it go as it was late and I really didn't want to deal with anyone for at least this evening. I reluctantly stumbled down the stairs to the door and opened to find our lawyer standing there with a letter in his hand.

"I am sorry, Collin, but I had to bring this over as soon as I saw it."

"Saw what?"

"The letter."

"What letter?"

"The letter Ava left in her last will and testament. I didn't see it before, but when I was going over everything again, I saw it and had to get it to you."

I took the letter and promised to call him the next day. I closed the door and walked slowly back up the stairs, trying to imagine what it said.

Finally, I opened the letter and read the final words Ava left to us, her family.

Hey, Baby,

If you're reading this, I guess I beat you home. As always, I won. Please know I was blessed to be your wife. Tell my children I love them more than the life I lived, and I will always be with them and you. Collin, believe in who God made you to be, and don't let your gift go unnoticed but make it known that God uses all of us. I love you so much, and I will be waiting on you, I promise. Enjoy every day with our children, and live life to the fullest. You are and will always be my best friend, my confidante, and most of all the love of my life. Remember my favorite love story will always be ours.

THE END

Other book by this author:

A. Nobody

CPSIA information can be obtained at www.ICGtesting.com
Printed in the USA
LVOW05s2246091214

418044LV00003B/12/P